TOP
10
OF
BRITAIN

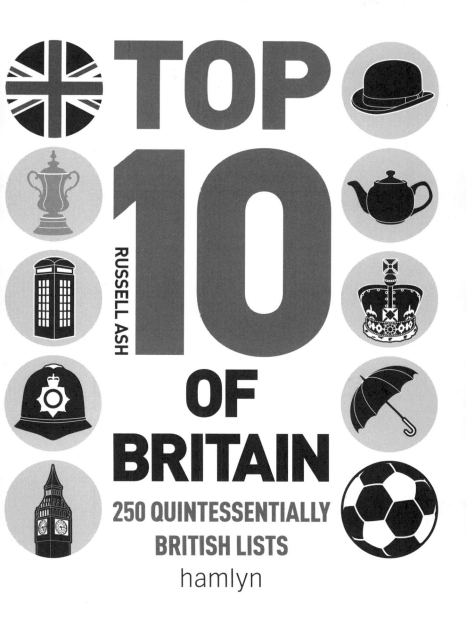

RUSSELL ASH

TOP 10

OF BRITAIN

250 QUINTESSENTIALLY BRITISH LISTS

hamlyn

Y941

An Hachette UK Company
www.hachette.co.uk

First published in Great Britain in 2009 by
Hamlyn, a division of Octopus Publishing Group Ltd
2–4 Heron Quays, London E14 4JP
www.octopusbooks.co.uk

ISBN 978-0-600-61921-5

A CIP catalogue record for this book is available from the
British Library

Printed and bound in China

10 9 8 7 6 5 4 3 2 1

Executive Editor Trevor Davies
Managing Editor Clare Churly
Deputy Creative Director Geoff Fennell
Page make-up Dorchester Typesetting Group Ltd
Production Manager David Hearn

CONTENTS

INTRODUCTION

'Britain, Britain …'

… as the introduction to a popular TV comedy series goes. I have been compiling the annual *Top 10 of Everything* for 20 years. In that and related books (Top 10s of Music, Sport and Film and *Top 10 for Men*) there is inevitably a fair crop of British lists, but this is the first time I have attempted to bring them together under one roof, as well as introduce a range of subjects that would probably never find a home in *Top 10 of Everything*. In *Top 10 of Everything* I have rigidly adhered to a rule I set for myself at the start, which was to ensure that every list in the book was quantifiable in one way or another (biggest, fastest, richest, or whatever) – if you can't measure it, it doesn't go in. In the derived books I am less strict about this, and so I have included numerous British lists of 10 that neatly encapsulate a theme, where ranking them is either impossible or serves no purpose.

'Green and pleasant land'

Much of what follows rejoices in our landscape and tourist attractions, the country's stately homes, its hill figures and mazes, towers and churches, that very British structure the seaside pier and the phenomenon of the steam railway, many of which have been preserved by enthusiastic volunteers. As well as the first railways, Britain gave the world everything from Christmas cards to the stamps to post them. Few other countries would offer such historical depth and range of subjects: alongside the milestones, from Magna Carta to the Spanish Armada, the Norman Conquest to the Battle of Britain, this book features events that occurred on Friday the 13th, British ghost towns, freak weather and our passion for time capsules, the English 'Season' and Women's Institutes. It is a country in which we encounter schools and universities dating back to the medieval period, companies founded over 300 years ago and bygone professions – most of which you wouldn't have wished to have follow. Its past also has a dark side that figures prominently: bloody battles, highwaymen, robbers, spies, unsolved murders and executions, along with its myths and legends, such as the Knights of the Round Table, as well as historical (and sometimes hysterical) epitaphs. There is an inevitable patriotic bias, and I make no apology for including lists relating to great British songs, Victoria Cross winners and national heroes from Shakespeare to Churchill.

'English eccentrics'

The title of a 1933 book by Edith Sitwell (herself no slouch in the English eccentric stakes) is apposite for many of the lists you will find in these pages: exotic folk customs, curious laws, weird words, silly names, bizarre books, peculiar museums, haunted houses and crazed End of the World prophets are among many categories that show Britain at its oddest. In conducting my research I have made such quirkily serendipitous discoveries as that the Museum of Dog Collars prohibits dogs, it is illegal to die in the Houses of Parliament, Florence Nightingale's pet owl has been preserved, Jane Austen mentioned baseball in *Northanger Abbey*, while I have tracked the transient life of Water Raleigh's head, found that 95 per cent of all British racehorses have DNA from 18th-century champion Eclipse and that Dickens's *Bleak House* originally had the less snappy title of *Tom-All-Alone's Factory that Got into Chancery and Never Got Out*. Should you get peckish along the way, you can feast on lists of traditional dishes from the Bedfordshire clanger to Stargazy pie, our favourite cheeses, sandwiches, snacks and biscuits, visit the foremost Michelin-starred restaurants and the longest-named pubs and consider the banquet at which guests who said 'I could eat a horse' had their wishes fulfilled.

'The British are coming!'

... bellowed Colin Welland as he picked up his Oscar (for writing *Chariots of Fire*) at the 1982 Academy Awards, and indeed there is plenty to celebrate in British film-making in lists featuring *James Bond*, *Carry On* and other British films, actors and directors, as well as British TV sitcoms, *Monty Python*, *Blue Peter*, our successes (and failures) at the Eurovision Song Contest and Christmas singles, not to mention the Top 10 singles banned by the BBC. Film and music lists are, incidentally, unless otherwise stated, ranked according to global box office earnings (or rental income for early releases) or sales, although precise figures, such as for record sales and those of duty free goods, are commercially confidential.

United Kingdom?

With apologies for this somewhat pedantic excursion, the terms 'Britain', 'British' and 'Briton' are used throughout to refer to people, places and events in Britain or the United Kingdom, or its components, England, Wales, Scotland and Northern Ireland as appropriate. The term 'Great Britain' was occasionally used from about 1603, and the Kingdom of Great Britain formed on 1 May 1707 when the kingdoms of England and Scotland were merged. On 1 January 1801, Ireland was included to form the United Kingdom of Great Britain and Ireland. After Irish independence (6 December 1922), the name continued to be used until 12 April 1927, when it became United Kingdom of Great Britain and Northern Ireland – which is the name that is used today, the wording that, for example, appears on a British passport (and repeated in Welsh and Gaelic). Although, since 1975, the terms 'Britain' and 'British' have been legally regarded as referring to the United Kingdom and its inhabitants, in the Internet Age the top-level domain for the country was established as .uk, not .gb. Conversely, while Great Britain is a geographical area comprising England, Wales and Scotland, but excluding Northern Ireland, the official International Olympic Committee abbreviation for Great Britain and Northern Ireland was established in 1908 as 'GBR' – at the 2008 Beijing Olympics popularly known as 'Team GB' – so in the sports section you will find entries variously referring to GB, GBR and the UK, all of which denote athletes from Great Britain and Northern Ireland.

Source material

Aside from my own reference library, I gather my data from a diverse range of official organizations, commercial companies and research bodies, specialized publications and a number of experts around the world, to all of whom I offer my warmest thanks (see page 304 for a full list of credits).

Please send me any comments or corrections and ideas for lists to the official Top 10 site – www.top10ofeverything.com or to my website www.RussellAsh.com.

Russell Ash

WHAT
MAKES
BRITAIN?

HIGHEST MOUNTAINS
in the UK

	Mountain	Height
1	Ben Nevis, Highland	1,344 m (4,408 ft)
2	Ben Macdhui, Moray	1,309 m (4,296 ft)
3	Braeriach, Aberdeenshire/Highland	1,296 m (4,252 ft)
4	Cairn Toul, Aberdeenshire	1,293 m (4,241 ft)
5	Cairn Gorm, Moray/Highland	1,245 m (4,084 ft)
6	Aonach Beag, Highland	1,236 m (4,054 ft)
7	Cairn Mor Dearg, Highland	1,223 m (4,012 ft)
8	Aonach Mor, Highland	1,219 m (3,999 ft)
9	Ben Lawers, Perth and Kinross	1,214 m (3,984 ft)
10	Beinn a' Bhuird, Aberdeenshire	1,196 m (3,924 ft)

All 10 of the UK's tallest mountains are in Scotland. The tallest in England, Wales and Northern Ireland respectively are:

• England: Scafell Pike (977 m/3,206 ft),
• Wales: Snowdon (1,085 m/3,560 ft)
• Northern Ireland: Slieve Donard (852 m/2,795 ft)

There are 284 mountains in Scotland over 914 m (3,000 ft). They are known as Munros after Sir Hugh Thomas Munro, who catalogued them in 1891. Enthusiastic mountaineers compete to climb as many of them as possible during their climbing careers.

LONGEST RIVERS
in the UK

	River	Length
1	Severn	354 km (220 miles)
2	Thames	346 km (215 miles)
3	Trent	297 km (185 miles)
4	Great Ouse	230 km (143 miles)
5	Wye	215 km (135 miles)
6	Ure/Ouse, Yorkshire	208 km (129 miles)
7	Tay	188 km (117 miles)
8	Clyde	176 km (109 miles)
9	Spey	172 km (107 miles)
10	Tweed	156 km (97 miles)

During their courses, some rivers change their names: for example, Trent/Humber, Thames/Isis.

LARGEST LAKES
in the UK

	Lake	Area
1	Lough Neagh, Northern Ireland	381.74 sq km (147.39 sq miles)
2	Lower Lough Erne, Northern Ireland	105.08 sq km (40.57 sq miles)
3	Loch Lomond, Scotland	71.12 sq km (27.46 sq miles)
4	Loch Ness, Scotland	56.64 sq km (21.87 sq miles)
5	Upper Lough Erne, Northern Ireland	42.99 sq km (16.6 sq miles)
6	Loch Awe, Scotland	38.72 sq km (14.95 sq miles)
7	Loch Maree, Scotland	28.49 sq km (11 sq miles)
8	Loch Morar, Scotland	26.68 sq km (10.3 sq miles)
9	Loch Tay, Scotland	26.39 sq km (10.19 sq miles)
10	Loch Shin, Scotland	22.53 sq km (8.7 sq miles)

The largest lake in England is Windermere at 14.74 sq km (5.69 sq miles) and the largest in Wales is Lake Vyrnwy at 8.24 sq km (3.18 sq miles). The largest manmade lake is Rutland Water at 12.59 sq km (4.86 sq miles). Despite being the largest by area, Lough Neagh is relatively shallow, with a maximum depth of 25 m (82 ft). Loch Morar is the deepest at 310 m (1,017 ft), followed by Loch Ness at 230 m (754 ft).

HIGHEST WATERFALLS
in the UK

	Waterfall	Total drop
1	Eas a' Chàul Aluinn, Scotland	201 m (658 ft)
2	Cautley Spout, England	198 m (650 ft)
3	Pystill Gwyn, Wales	152 m (500 ft)
4	Barvick Falls, Scotland	150 m (492 ft)
5	Falls of Buchan Burn, Scotland	135 m (443 ft)
6=	Rhaeadr y Cwm, Wales	122 m (400 ft)
=	Rhaeadr Myherin, Wales	122 m (400 ft)
8	An Steall Ban, Scotland	120 m (395 ft)
9	Falls of Glomach, Scotland	113 m (370 ft)
10	Pistyll Blaen y Cwm, Wales	107 m (350 ft)

TOP 10

LONGEST CANALS
in the UK

	Canal/year completed	Locks	Tunnels	Length
1	Grand Union (main line), 1814	166	2	220.5 km (137 miles)
2	Leeds and Liverpool, 1816	93	2	204.4 km (127 miles)
3	Trent and Mersey, 1777	73	4	149.7 km (93 miles)
4	Kennet and Avon, 1810	106	1	139.2 km (86.5 miles)
5	Oxford, 1790	43	1	123.9 km (77 miles)
6	Shropshire Union, 1805	47	0	107 km (66.5 miles)
7	Caledonian, 1822	29	0	96.6 km (60 km)
8	Staffordshire and Worcestershire, 1772	45	0	74.2 km (46.1 miles)
9	Llangollen, 1805	21	2	74 km (46 miles)
10	Lancaster, 1799	0	0	68.4 km (42.5 miles)

Source: British Waterways

LARGEST ISLANDS
in the UK

	Island/location	Area
1	Lewis and Harris, Outer Hebrides, Scotland	2,225.3 sq km (859.19 sq miles)
2	Skye, Hebrides, Scotland	1,666.08 sq km (643.27 sq miles)
3	Mainland, Shetland, Scotland	967 sq km (373.36 sq miles)
4	Mull, Inner Hebrides, Scotland	899.25 sq km (347.2 sq miles)
5	Ynys Môn (Anglesey), Wales	713.8 sq km (275.6 sq miles)
6	Islay, Inner Hebrides, Scotland	638.79 sq km (246.64 sq miles)
7	Isle of Man, England	571.66 sq km (220.72 sq miles)
8	Mainland, Orkney, Scotland	536.1 sq km (206.99 sq miles)
9	Arran, Inner Hebrides, Scotland	435.32 sq km (168.08 sq miles)
10	Isle of Wight, England	380.99 sq km (147.1 sq miles)

LARGEST FORESTS
in the UK

	Forest*	Area
1	Galloway Forest Park, Dumfries and Galloway	770 sq km (297 sq miles)
2	Kielder Forest Park, Northumberland	610 sq km (235 sq miles)
3	New Forest, Hampshire	270 sq km (104 sq miles)
4	Dornoch Forest, Sutherland	260 sq km (100 sq miles)
5	Argyll Forest Park, Argyll	210 sq km (81 sq miles)
6	Queen Elizabeth Forest Park, Stirling	200 sq km (77 sq miles)
7	Thetford Forest Park, Norfolk/Suffolk	190 sq km (73 sq miles)
8	Affric Forest (Fort Augustus), Inverness-shire	180 sq km (69 sq miles)
9	Tay Forest Park, Perthshire	170 sq km (65 sq miles)
10	Glengarry Forest (Lochaber Forest District), Inverness-shire	165 sq km (63 sq miles)

* Forestry Commission forests, including areas designated as Forest Parks, which can include areas not covered by woodland
Source: Forestry Commission

ANCIENT BRITISH ROADS AND ROUTES

1 **Akeman Street**
   The Roman road that connected London to the Fosse Way at Cirencester. Today the A41 follows part of its route.

2 **Dere Street**
   This Roman road joined York and the Antonine Wall in Scotland.

3 **Ermine Street**
   An important Roman road from London to York, now partly followed by the A1.

4 **Fosse Way**
   The Roman road from Exeter to Lincoln follows a remarkably straight line. Several place names on its route derive from those of Roman military camps.

5 **Harrow Way**
   Part of a Neolithic trackway from the Dover area to Stonehenge and beyond to Cornwall.

6 **Icknield Way**
   This East Anglian route existed before the arrival of the Romans.

7 **Pilgrims' Way**
   The route used by medieval pilgrims from Winchester, Hampshire, to the shrine of Thomas Becket in Canterbury, Kent.

8 **Sarn Helen**
   A Roman road in Wales connecting Aberconwy and Carmarthen, a distance of some 257 km (160 miles).

9 **The Ridgeway**
   Considered one of Britain's most ancient roads, its 147-km (85-mile) route connects Overton Hill near Avebury, Wiltshire, and Ivinghoe Beacon, Buckinghamshire.

10 **Watling Street**
   This road was used by the Celts. The section between London and Dover was paved by the Romans and became the present-day A2.

LONGEST MOTORWAYS
in the UK

	Motorway	Route	Length
1	M6	Rugby–Carlisle	364.8 km (226.7 miles)
2	M1	London–Leeds	307.1 km (190.8 miles)
3	M4	London–Pont Abraham	305 km (189.5 miles)
4	M5	Birmingham–Exeter	262.2 km (162.9 miles)
5	M25	Circles London	188.3 km (117 miles)
6	M62	Liverpool–Humberside	173.3 km (107.7 miles)
7	M40	Birmingham–London	143.2 km (89 miles)
8	M3	London–Southampton	94.3 km (58.6 miles)
9	M11	London–Cambridge	80 km (49.7 miles)
10	M8	Edinburgh–Glasgow Airport	78.4 km (48.7 miles)

Britain's first motorway was the Preston bypass section of the M6 (between junctions 29 and 32), which opened on 5 December 1958. The first section of the M1 did not open until 2 November 1959.

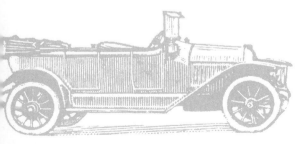

MOST COMMON PLACE NAMES
in Britain

	Name	Number of occurrences
1	Newton	150
2	Blackhill/Black Hill	136
3	Castlehill/Castle Hill	128
4	Mountpleasant/Mount Pleasant	126
5	Woodside/Wood Side	112
6	Newtown/New Town	110
7	Burnside	107
8	Greenhill/Green Hill	105
9	Woodend/Wood End	101
10	Beacon Hill	95

Source: Ordnance Survey
These entries include the names of towns, villages and other inhabited settlements, as
well as woods, hills and named locations, but exclude combinations of these names
with others (Newton Abbot and Newton-le-Willows, for example, are not counted with
the Newtons).

UNUSUAL PLACE NAMES
in the UK

1 **Backside**
Grampian, Scotland, boasts two locations called Backside, while North Yorkshire has a Backsides.

2 **Balls**
As well as Balls, Devon has a Balls Corner and a Balls Cross.

3 **Crackpot**
The name of Crackpot, a village in Swaledale, North Yorkshire, probably relates to a pothole in the local limestone.

4 **Great Snoring**
Formerly Snoring Magna, Norfolk's village is believed to have been named after a local inhabitant called Snaer. It is near Little Snoring, which is actually bigger.

5 **Jump**
The South Yorkshire village of Jump claims to owe its name to a stream that ran through it over which locals had to leap.

6 **Nasty**
The Hertfordshire hamlet's name comes from the Old English for '(place at) the east enclosure'.

7 **New Invention**
Places with this name are found in the West Midlands, first recorded in 1663, and in Shropshire and Somerset. It may come from a machine used in local mines.

8 **Pity Me**
Both Durham and Northumberland have villages of this name. Some say it is a translation of *Miserere mei* (Psalm 51), sung by monks during the Viking invasions, but more probably it derives from Pithead Mere, the marshy wasteland near a coal mine.

9 **Splatt**
The village of Splatt lies between Pityme and Rock, Cornwall. There are also Splatts in Devon and Somerset.

10 **Thong**
Britain's one and only Thong is in Kent. The name is said to come from the Old English *thwang*, a narrow strip of land.

TOP 10

HOUSE NAMES
in the UK

1 The Cottage

2 Rose Cottage

3 The Bungalow

4 The Coach House

5 Orchard House

6 The Lodge

7 Woodlands

8 The Old School House

9 Ivy Cottage

10 The Willows

Source: HBOS

TOP 10

LARGEST BRITISH COUNTIES*

	County	Area
1	Highland, Scotland	25,659 sq km (9,907 sq miles)
2	North Yorkshire, England	8,038 sq km (3,103 sq miles)
3	Argyll and Bute, Scotland	6,909 sq km (2,668 sq miles)
4	Cumbria, England	6,768 sq km (2,613 sq miles)
5	Devon, England	6,564 sq km (2,534 sq miles)
6	Dumfries and Galloway, Scotland	6,426 sq km (2,481 sq miles)
7	Aberdeenshire, Scotland	6,313 sq km (2,437 sq miles)
8	Lincolnshire, England	5,921 sq km (2,286 sq miles)
9	Norfolk, England	5,371 sq km (2,074 sq miles)
10	Perth and Kinross, Scotland	5,286 sq km (2,041 sq miles)

* Scotland = council areas
Source: National Statistics
Powys is the largest Welsh principal area at 5,196 sq km (2,006 sq miles) and Tyrone the largest in Northern Ireland at 3,155 sq km (1,218 sq miles).

SMALLEST BRITISH COUNTIES*

	County	Area
1	City of Dundee, Scotland	60 sq km (23 sq miles)
2	Blaenau Gwent, Wales	109 sq km (42 sq miles)
3	Merthyr Tydfil, Wales	111 sq km (43 sq miles)
4	Torfaen, Wales	126 sq km (49 sq miles)
5	Cardiff, Wales	140 sq km (54 sq miles)
6=	Clackmannanshire, Scotland	159 sq km (61 sq miles)
=	West Dunbartonshire, Scotland	159 sq km (61 sq miles)
8	Inverclyde, Scotland	160 sq km (62 sq miles)
9	East Renfrewshire, Scotland	174 sq km (67 sq miles)
10	City of Glasgow, Scotland	175 sq km (68 sq miles)

* Scotland = council areas
Source: National Statistics
As a result of local government reorganization of its traditional counties, Scotland now has both the largest and some of the smallest council areas in the UK. The smallest county in England (excluding unitary authorities) is Bedfordshire at 1,192 sq km (460 sq miles).

MOST DENSELY POPULATED COUNTIES in the UK

	County	Population
1	West Midlands	2,884 per sq km (7,470 per sq mile)
2	Merseyside	2,099 per sq km (5,436 per sq mile)
3	Tyne and Wear	2,014 per sq km (5,216 per sq mile)
4	Greater Manchester	2,001 per sq km (5,183 per sq mile)
5	West Yorkshire	1,065 per sq km (2,758 per sq mile)
6	South Yorkshire	883 per sq km (2,287 per sq mile)
7	Surrey	653 per sq km (1,691 per sq mile)
8	Hertfordshire	644 per sq km (1,668 per sq mile)
9	Lancashire	402 per sq km (1,041 per sq mile)
10	Essex	393 per sq km (1,018 per sq mile)

Source: National Statistics
This list includes metropolitan counties (created 1974), but excludes Scottish council areas. Although it lost its county status in 1965, Greater London has a population density of 4,779 per sq km (12,378 per sq mile). Within its borders, the most over-crowded piece of land in England is Kensington and Chelsea, London, where each of its 12 sq kms (4.6 sq miles) accommodates 14,676 people per sq km (38,011 per sq mile).

LEAST DENSELY POPULATED
COUNTIES* in the UK

County	Population
1 Powys	25 per sq km (65 per sq mile)
2 Ceredigion	43 per sq km (111 per sq mile)
3 Gwynedd	47 per sq km (122 per sq mile)
4 Northumberland	62 per sq km (161 per sq mile)
5 Pembrokeshire	72 per sq km (186 per sq mile)
6 Cumbria	73 per sq km (189 per sq mile)
7 North Yorkshire	74 per sq km (192 per sq mile)
8 Carmarthenshire	75 per sq km (194 per sq mile)
9 Shropshire	90 per sq km (233 per sq mile)
10 Isle of Anglesey	97 per sq km (251 per sq mile)

* Excluding Scottish council areas
Source: National Statistics

TOP10

OLDEST CITIES
in the UK

	City	Original charter granted
1	Ripon	886
2	London	1066
3	Edinburgh	1124
4	Chichester	1135
5=	Lincoln	1154
=	Oxford	1154
7=	Nottingham	1155
=	Winchester	1155
9	Exeter	1156
10	Carlisle	1158

There are 66 cities in the UK. Although most of them were settled in earlier times, some as far back as the first century BC, their status as cities is dated from when their charters, issued by the Crown and establishing certain privileges, such as the power to enact local laws or collect taxes, were granted. Some dates are disputed: Norwich, for example, claims to have received its original charter in 996, but 1194 is the more accepted date. Some, such as Canterbury and Durham, have claimed city status for centuries, but, contrary to popular belief, not all cities have cathedrals. Southampton, for example, does not, while, conversely, St David's has a cathedral but did not gain a city charter until 1995. Chelmsford, St Asaph, Bury St Edmunds and Blackburn all have cathedrals but have yet to achieve city status, while Rochester, Perth and Elgin are no longer classed as cities.

LARGEST CITIES IN BRITAIN
1801–2001[*]

	1801 City	Population	2001 City	Population
1	London	1,096,784	London†	7,172,036
2	Manchester	328,609	Birmingham	977,091
3	Edinburgh	82,560	Leeds	715,404
4	Liverpool	82,430	Glasgow	577,869
5	Glasgow	77,385	Sheffield	513,234
6	Birmingham	70,207	Bradford	467,668
7	Bristol	63,645	Edinburgh	448,624
8	Portsmouth	43,461	Liverpool	439,476
9	Plymouth	43,194	Manchester	392,918
10	Newcastle	36,963	Kirklees	388,576

* Cities only, excluding conurbations
† Complete area: Inner London 2,765,975; Outer London 4,406,061
Taking the populations of cities only as at the censuses of 1801 and 2001 disregards the colossal growth of conurbations in the 200 years that separates them: the total 2001 population of Greater Manchester (including Bolton, Stockport, Wigan and other places), for example, totalled 2,482,352.

LOST TOWNS AND VILLAGES
of Britain

1 **Ashopton, Derbyshire**
Along with the village of Derwent, Ashopton was submerged when the Ladybower Reservoir was built in 1943.

2 **Dunwich, Suffolk**
Once a prosperous port, Dunwich has been progressively lost to the sea, with most of its houses and churches now under water.

3 **Godwick, Norfolk**
Abandoned in the late 16th century, Godwick is today managed by English Heritage and is open to the public.

4 **Gruinard Island, Scotland**
In 1942 the 195-hectare (483-acre) island was evacuated and used for testing anthrax biological warfare. It has since been decontaminated, but remains unpopulated.

5 **Hallsands, Devon**
Dredging of materials from the beach destabilized the coast, causing the houses to collapse into the sea, so that by 1917 it was uninhabited.

6 **Imber, Wiltshire**
Imber on Salisbury Plain was requisitioned by the army in 1943 and used for street-fighting training. The public are occasionally allowed to visit the deserted village.

7 **Polphail Village, Argyllshire**
Polphail was built to house North Sea oil platform workers in 1976, but was never occupied.

8 **Tide Mills, East Sussex**
The village near Newhaven once housed workers in the adjoining tide-powered mill. The mill ceased operating in the early 20th century and by 1939 the settlement was abandoned.

9 **Tyneham, Dorset**
Tyneham's 200 inhabitants were evicted in 1943 when the village was taken over for use as a firing range. Parts have been preserved and it is now open to the public.

10 **Wharram Percy, Yorkshire**
The desertion of this medieval village was once blamed on the Black Death, but now seems more the result of changes in land use. Only its church remains – as does that of Wolfhampcote on the border of Warwickshire and Northamptonshire, which appears to have suffered the same fate.

TOP 10

WETTEST PLACES
in Britain

	Weather station	Average annual rainfall
1	Dalness, Glen Etive, Highland	3,306 mm (130.16 in)
2	Seathwaite, nr Borrowdale, Cumbria	3,150 mm (124.02 in)
3	Glenfinnan, Loch Shiel, Highland	3,022 mm (118.98 in)
4	Inverarnan, Loch Lomond, Stirling	2,701 mm (106.34 in)
5	Inveruglas, Loch Lomond, Argyll and Bute	2,662 mm (104.8 in)
6	Capel Curig, Gwynedd	2,555 mm (100.59 in)
7	Wythburn, Lake Thirlmere, Cumbria	2,535 mm (99.8 in)
8=	Chapel Stile, Cumbria	2,500 mm (98.43 in)
=	Tyndrum and Crianlarich, Stirling	2,500 mm (98.43 in)
10	Lochgoilhead, Argyll and Bute	2,464 mm (97.01 in)

Source: The Met Office
These figures are based on the Meteorological Office's 30-year averages for the period 1961–90 and are for the wettest inhabited places (villages and towns) in Great Britain. It should be noted, though, that some uninhabited places in the mountainous parts of Scotland, North Wales and Cumbria are wetter, with annual average rainfall in excess of 3,500 mm (137.8 in).

WETTEST YEARS
in England and Wales

	Year	Total rainfall
1	1872	1,288 mm (50.70 in)
2	1852	1,266 mm (49.84 in)
3	1768	1,192 mm (46.92 in)
4	1960	1,171 mm (46.10 in)
5	1903	1,147 mm (45.15 in)
6	1882	1,135 mm (44.68 in)
7	1877	1,134 mm (44.64 in)
8	1848	1,130 mm (44.48 in)
9	1841	1,120 mm (44.09 in)
10	1912	1,118 mm (44.01 in)

Source: The Met Office
British meteorologist George Symons (1838–1900), the author of *Rain: How, When, Where, Why It Is Measured* (1867), published a table of rainfall for the period 1726–1865, listing 1852 as the wettest year. In 1872, this was beaten by an average annual rainfall that holds the record to this day. In modern times (the 30-year period 1971–2000), the annual average for England and Wales was 920.7 mm (36.2 in), for Scotland 1,521 mm (59.9 in), for Northern Ireland 1,112.3 mm (43.79 in) and for the UK as a whole 1,126.1 mm (44.33 in).

WARMEST PLACES
in the UK

	Location	Average annual temperature*
1	St Helier Harbour, Jersey	12.1°C (53.8°F)
2	St Mary's Airport, Isles of Scilly	11.9°C (53.4°F)
3=	St Helier, Jersey	11.8°C (53.2°F)
=	Lancresse, Guernsey	11.8°C (53.2°F)
5=	Central London	11.7°C (53.1°F)
=	Round Island, Isles of Scilly	11.7°C (53.1°F)
7	St Mary's, Isles of Scilly	11.6°C (52.9°F)
8=	Pendennis Point, Cornwall	11.4°C (52.5°F)
=	St James's Park, London	11.4°C (52.5°F)
10=	Greenwich, London	11.3°C (52.3°F)
=	Isle of Grain, Kent	11.3°C (52.3°F)
=	Penlee Gardens, Penzance	11.3°C (52.3°F)
=	Portland, Dorset	11.3°C (52.3°F)
=	Ryde, Isle of Wight	11.3°C (52.3°F)
=	St Ives, Cornwall	11.3°C (52.3°F)
=	Southsea, Hampshire	11.3°C (52.3°F)

* Based on the Met Office's 30-year averages for the period 1971–2000
Source: The Met Office

EXTREME AND WEIRD WEATHER EVENTS in the UK

1 ## Tornado
Tornadoes are rare in Britain, but one of the earliest recorded was that affecting London on 23 October 1091. It was also one of the worst: London Bridge was completely swept away, St Mary-le-Bow and other churches and as many as 600 houses were destroyed and the newly built Tower of London was damaged, but only two deaths were recorded.

2 ## Frost
One of the severest frosts of all time lasted from November 1683 until April 1684. The Thames was iced over from early December until 4 February and a massive 'Frost Fair' was held on it. The icebound river was turned into a bustling town as tradespeople erected booths on the ice. King Charles II visited the fair and watched bull-baiting, horse racing and puppet shows and took part in a fox hunt on the river. The winter of 1813–14 saw the last great Frost Fair, but when the ice melted suddenly, many booths and people were swept away. Old London Bridge acted as a barrier, slowing the flow and allowing ice to build up. It was demolished and a new bridge opened in 1831, since when the river has not frozen to its previous extent.

3 ## Lightning
On 27 October 1697 a massive lightning strike – or possibly a fireball – struck Athlone Castle, blowing up 260 barrels of gunpowder, 1,000 hand grenades, 220 barrels of musket and pistol balls and other munitions. The resulting fire destroyed most of the town, but killed only eight.

4 ## Sunblock
Tambora, a volcano in Indonesia, erupted on 5–12 April 1815. An estimated 1.7 million tonnes of ash was hurled into the atmosphere, which, during the following year, blocked out the sunlight and affected the weather over large areas of the globe, including Britain, with 1816 being known as 'the year without a summer'. One effect was to produce brilliantly coloured sunsets, depicted strikingly in paintings from the period, especially in the works of J. M. W. Turner. It even had an influence on literary history: kept indoors by inclement weather at the Villa Diodati on Lake Geneva, Lord Byron and his companions amused themselves by writing horror stories, one of which was Mary Shelley's classic, *Frankenstein*.

5 Avalanche

Britain's avalanche occurred in Lewes, East Sussex, on 27 December 1836, engulfing houses and killing eight. The disaster is commemorated in the name of the Snowdrop pub.

6 Blizzard

A severe blizzard on 9 March 1891 left *Zulu*, an express train, trapped in snow on Dartmoor for four days before the passengers were rescued. Some passengers, along with the drivers and guard, stayed with the train, which finally arrived at Plymouth eight days late.

7 Storm surge

A huge storm surge down the North Sea coast from Yorkshire to Kent on 31 January–1 February 1953 resulted in flooding that left 307 dead and 30,000 homeless. During the storm, the ferry MV *Princess Victoria* sank en route from Stranraer, Scotland to Larne, Northern Ireland, with the loss of 133 lives. As a result of the catastrophe, British coastal defences were improved and plans launched for building the Thames Barrier.

8 Rain of frogs

Thousands of baby frogs fell in a sudden downpour in Sutton Coldfield, Warwickshire, on 12 June 1954.

9 Rainfall

On the night of 18–19 July 1955 at Martinstown, Dorset, a record 279 mm (11 in) of rain fell in a continuous downpour.

10 Storm

The great storm of 15–16 October 1987 left 22 dead and destroyed 14 million trees across southern England. There were 1.2 million insurance claims totalling over £1.5 billion, making it the most expensive natural disaster to date.

HOTTEST YEARS
in the UK*

	Year	Average temperature
1	2006	10.82°C (51.48°F)
2=	1990	10.63°C (51.13°F)
=	1999	10.63°C (51.13°F)
4	1949	10.62°C (51.12°F)
5	2002	10.6°C (51.08°F)
6	1995	10.53°C (50.95°F)
7	1997	10.52°C (50.94°F)
8=	1989	10.5°C (50.9°F)
=	2003	10.5°C (50.9°F)
10=	1959	10.48°C (50.86°F)
=	2004	10.48°C (50.86°F)
=	2007	10.48°C (50.86°F)

* Since 1659, based on central England averages
Source: The Met Office
Temperature has been recorded in central England since 1659, providing the world's longest span of temperature data. In the 17th century the warmest year was 1686 (10.13°C/50.23°F); in the 18th century it was 1733 and in the 19th century it was 1834 (both 10.47°C/50.85°F).

THE PEOPLE
OF BRITAIN

TOP 10
OLDEST BRITISH-BORN PEOPLE

	Name/dates	Age Years	Months	Days
1	Charlotte Hughes* (1 Aug 1877–17 Mar 1993)	115	7	16
2	Annie Jennings (12 Nov 1884–20 Nov 1999)	115	0	8
3	Eva Morris* (8 Nov 1885–2 Nov 2000)	114	11	25
4	Anna Eliza Williams* (2 Jun 1873–27 Dec 1987)	114	6	25
5	Grace Clawson (15 Nov 1887–28 May 2002)	114	6	13
6	Lucy Jane Askew* (8 Sep 1883–9 Dec 1997)	114	3	1
7	Amy Isabel Hulmes (5 Oct 1887–27 Oct 2001)	114	0	22
8	Rosa Ann Comfort (21 Jan 1879–6 Nov 1992)	113	9	16
9	Daisy Adams* (30 Jun 1880–8 Dec 1993)	113	6	8
10	Florence Finch (22 Dec 1893–10 Apr 2007)	113	3	19

* Held record as Britain's oldest living person

This list is based on the longevity of British people for whom there is undisputed evidence of their date of birth. Even the oldest falls almost seven years short of the 122-year, 5-month and 15-day lifespan of Jeanne Calment of France, who lived from 21 February 1875 to 4 August 1997. The oldest confirmed age of a British man is the 112 years, 9 months and 22 days of Welsh-born John Evans, who lived from 19 August 1877 to 10 June 1990.

HEAVIEST PEOPLE
in the UK

	Name/location/dates	Peak weight
1=	Barry Austin (Birmingham, b. 1971)	413 kg (65 st)
=	Christopher Alan McGarva (Lincoln, 1969–2005)	413 kg (65 st)
3	Peter Yarnall (London, 1949–84)	375 kg (59 st)
4	Jack Taylor (Bradford, Yorkshire, c.1945–2006)	357 kg (56 st)
5	William Campbell (Glasgow, 1856–78)	340 kg (53 st 8 lb)
6	Daniel Lambert (Leicester, 1770–1809)	335 kg (52 st 11 lb)
7=	Roger Byrne (Rosenallis, Ireland, ?–1808)	330 kg (52 st)
=	Nicholas Sturley (Lowestoft, Suffolk, b. 1966)	330 kg (52 st)
9	Melvin Jones (Bangor, Wales, 1934–88)	324 kg (51 st)
10	Martin Ruane (aka 'Giant Haystacks'; London, 1947–88)	318 kg (50 st)

Many claims of extreme weight – such as one of a G. Hopkins of Wales, who in the late 18th century was said to be 445 kg (70 st) – are exaggerated. Those in this Top 10 are reliably documented, but difficulties in weighing extremely heavy people mean that some weights may be estimates.

TALLEST BRITISH PEOPLE

Name/dates	Height

1   **Patrick Cotter (O'Brien) (*c.*1760–18 Sep 1806)**   **246.4 cm (8 ft 1 in)**
Irish-born Patrick Cotter claimed a height of 262 cm (8 ft 7 in), but this was probably an exaggeration to attract customers to his personal appearances. When he stood on the stage at Sadler's Wells Theatre, London, he was said to have been able to reach into the boxes, and in the street he amazed onlookers by lighting his pipe from the gas jets of street lamps. When he died, he was buried in Bristol – 3.6 m (12 ft) deep and bricked in to deter bodysnatchers.

2   **Jane Bunford (1895–1922)**   **241.3 cm (7 ft 11 in)**
Jane Bunford of Bartley Green, Northfield, Birmingham, suffered from curvature of the spine, so it was never possible to measure her accurately, but she was the tallest British woman ever, and probably the world's tallest in her lifetime. Her memorial at Bartley Green Library confirms her height as 241.3 cm (7 ft 11 in).

3   **Charles O'Brien (or Byrne) (1761–83)**   **238.8 cm (7 ft 10 in)**
A height of 248.9 cm (8 ft 2 in) was claimed by Charles Byrne, who, like Cotter, was Irish and similarly adopted the name O'Brien. Although he asked to be buried at sea, his skeleton was acquired by Dr William Hunter, a British surgeon, and is on display in the Hunterian Museum at the Royal College of Surgeons, London, along with his giant gloves and other personal items.

4=   **Angus MacAskill (1825–63)**   **236.2 cm (7 ft 9 in)**
MacAskill was born at Dunvegan, Isle of Skye and emigrated to Nova Scotia as a child. By his 20th year, he was 224 cm (7 ft 4 in) tall, soon reaching his peak height and a weight of 263 kg (580 lb). His shoulders were 112 cm (44 in) across and his hands 20 cm (8 in) wide and 30 cm (12 in) long, with shoes measured 48 cm (19 in) long. He appeared with Phineas T. Barnum's circus, demonstrating feats of great strength, and gave a command performance for Queen Victoria. Museums dedicated to MacAskill have been established in Nova Scotia and at his birthplace.

=   **John Middleton (1578–1623)**   **236.2 cm (7 ft 9 in)**
Middleton's epitaph at Hale, near Liverpool, states 'Here lyeth the bodie of John Middleton the Childe of Hale. Nine feet three.' He visited the court of King James in 1620 and is commemorated by a portrait at Brasenose College, Oxford, which also has a painted outline of his giant hand, which Samuel Pepys describes in his *Diary*.

= **William Bradley (1787–1820)**   **236.2 cm (7 ft 9 in)**
Bradley, of Market Weighton, Yorkshire, was known as the 'Yorkshire Giant'. He was buried there within All Saints' Church to avoid the risk of bodysnatchers stealing his remains. A plaque with a life-sized footprint measuring 38 cm (15 in) is displayed in the town.

7= **Frederick John Kempster (1889–1918)**   **235 cm (7 ft 8½ in)**
Born in Bayswater, London, Kempster exhibited himself in fairs and circuses and acquired a multitude of nicknames, among them 'Fred, the Giant of Wiltshire' and 'The Blackburn Giant'. He died of pneumonia, aged 29, and was buried in a 274.3-cm (9-ft) coffin that required 10 pallbearers to carry and 14 to lower it into his grave.

= **Ernest Evans (1924–58)**   **235 cm (7 ft 8½ in)**
Ernest Edward 'Ted' Evans was born in Chesterfield, Derbyshire, and lived in Englefield Green, Surrey. He was widely claimed to be 274.3 cm (9 ft) and the 'tallest man alive'.

9 **Neil Fingleton (b. 1980)**   **232.4 cm (7 ft 7½ in)**
Britain's current record-holder spent several years as a basketball player in the USA, where he now lives.

10 **George Page (1844–70)**   **231.1 cm (7 ft 7 in)**
Billed as the 'Suffolk Giant', Page toured in a circus with his brother Meadows Page, who was a mere 223.5 cm (7 ft 4 in). Several other British men, including Albert Brough (1870–1919), (William) George Auger (1886–1922) and Henry Dalglish (1926–51), have claimed the same height.

TOP 10

ETHNIC GROUPS
in the UK

	Group	Percentage of total	Number*
1	White	92.1	54,153,898
2	Indian	1.8	1,053,411
3	Pakistani	1.3	747,285
4	Mixed	1.2	677,117
5	Black Caribbean	1	565,876
6	Black African	0.8	485,277
7	Bangladeshi	0.5	283,063
8	Other Asian	0.4	247,664
9	Chinese	0.4	247,403
10	Other ethnic group (not included elsewhere)	0.4	230,615
	Total (including 'Black other', 97,585)	*100*	*58,789,194*

* Based on the 2001 Census
Source: National Statistics

BRITISH DEMONYMS*

1   Birmingham – Brummy or Brummie
First used in print as recently as 1941, it derives from an earlier term, 'Brummagem', applied to locally made products.

2   Cambridge – Cantabrigian
A Cantabrigian – sometimes abbreviated to 'Tab' – is a member or former member of the University of Cambridge, from *Cantabrigia*, the Latin name for Cambridge.

3   Cornwall – Kernewek
Kernewek is Cornish for 'Cornish'. Although revived in recent years, the last native monoglot (single-language) speaker of the Cornish language died in 1777.

4   Grimsby – Grimbarian
First recorded in 1886, the term is considered more acceptable than the alternative, 'Codhead', a reference to the local fishing industry.

5   Leeds – Loiner
There are many explanations for the demonym 'Loiner', from the low inns around Briggate or the locals who loitered in the lanes, or 'loins'.

6   Liverpool – Scouse
The term 'lobscouse', a stew eaten by sailors, was applied in the 19th century to the sailors themselves, 'Scouse' first appearing in print as an alternative to 'Liverpudlian' in 1945.

7   Plymouth – Janner
A Janner is generally a person from the West Country, but has become closely associated with Plymouth, where it is sometimes used derogatively as a synonym for 'chav'.

8   Slough – Paludian
The name derives from the Latin *palus*, a slough or marsh.

9   Sunderland – Mackem or Maccam
One theory claims that it derives from the local shipbuilding industry, hence we 'make'em' ('make them').

10   York – Eboracian
The Roman name of the city was *Eburacum*, a 'place with many yew trees'. Anglo-Saxons adapted it to Eoforic (boar town) and the Vikings to Evorik/Jorvik, hence York.

* The members of a people or the inhabitants of a place.

TOP 10

WOMEN'S NAMES IN BRITISH HISTORY

	13th century	16th century	18th century	1900
1	Alice	Elizabeth	Mary	Mary
2	Matilda	Anne	Elizabeth	Florence
3	Joan	Joan	Ann	Doris
4	Agnes	Margaret	Sarah	Edith
5	Emma	Alice	Jane	Dorothy
6	Isabel(la)	Mary	Margaret	Annie
7	Margery	Agnes	Susan	Margaret
8	Cristian(i)a	Catherine	Martha	Alice
9	Ro(h)esia	Jane	Hannah	Elizabeth
10	Juliana	Dorothy	Catherine	Elsie

MEN'S NAMES IN BRITISH HISTORY

	13th century	16th century	18th century	1900
1	William	John	John	William
2	John	Thomas	William	John
3	Robert	William	Thomas	George
4	Richard	Richard	Richard	Thomas
5	Roger	Robert	James	Charles
6	Ralph	Henry	Robert	Frederick
7	Thomas	George	Joseph	Arthur
8	Henry	Edward	Edward	James
9	Geoffrey	Nicholas	Henry	Albert
10	Walter	James	George	Ernest

TOP 10
GIRLS' NAMES (2007)

	England	Wales	Scotland	Northern Ireland
1	Grace	Ruby	Sophie	Katie
2	Ruby	Megan	Emma	Grace
3	Olivia	Grace	Lucy	Sophie
4	Emily	Chloe	Katie	Lucy
5	Jessica	Emily	Erin	Emma
6	Sophie	Ffion	Ellie	Ellie
7	Chloe	Olivia	Amy	Sarah
8	Lily	Seren	Emily	Erin
9	Ellie	Ella	Chloe	Hannah
10	Amelia	Sophie	Olivia	Anna

TOP 10

BOYS' NAMES (2007)

	England	Wales	Scotland	Northern Ireland
1	Jack	Jack	Lewis	Jack
2	Thomas	Dylan	Jack	James
3	Oliver	Thomas	Ryan	Matthew
4	Joshua	Joshua	James	Daniel
5	Harry	Rhys	Callum	Ryan
6	Charlie	Daniel	Cameron	Thomas
7	Daniel	Ethan	Daniel	Adam
8	William	Oliver	Liam	Joshua
9	James	William	Jamie	Dylan
10	Alfie	James	Kyle	Ben

SURNAMES
in England and Wales

	Surname	Number
1	Smith	652,563
2	Jones	538,874
3	Williams	380,379
4	Taylor	306,296
5	Brown	291,872
6	Davies*	279,647
7	Evans	225,580
8	Thomas	202,773
9	Wilson	201,224
10	Johnson	193,260

* There are also 97,349 people with the surname Davis
This recent survey of British surnames is based on an analysis of 54.4 million appearing in the England and Wales electoral rolls – meaning only those aged over 18 and eligible to vote. Some 12 people out of every 1,000 in the UK are called Smith, compared with 14.55 in a sample from the 1851 Census. This decline may be accounted for by considering the diluting effect of immigrant names, the same survey indicating, for example, that 137,088 people, or 2.52 per 1,000, now bear the surname Patel, compared with just seven listed in 1851.

GREAT
BRITONS

TOP 10

GREATEST BRITONS

	Great Briton	Supporter
1	Sir Winston Churchill	Mo Mowlam
2	Isambard Kingdom Brunel	Jeremy Clarkson
3	Diana, Princess of Wales	Rosie Boycott
4	Charles Darwin	Andrew Marr
5	William Shakespeare	Fiona Shaw
6	Sir Isaac Newton	Tristram Hunt
7	Queen Elizabeth I	Michael Portillo
8	John Lennon	Alan Davies
9	Lord Nelson	Lucy Moore
10	Oliver Cromwell	Richard Holmes

In 2002 the BBC conducted a poll to discover the 100 Greatest Britons. Each of the Top 10 had a celebrity supporter, with viewers' votes providing the final ranking. Churchill received 447,423 votes, Brunel 391,262 and Diana 222,055.

OLD BRITISH ACHIEVERS

1 ## Queen Elizabeth II (b. 1926)
On 21 December 2007 Queen Elizabeth became Britain's oldest monarch at 81 years and 8 months, overtaking the 81-year, 7-month and 29-day lifespan of Queen Victoria.

2 ## George Bernard Shaw (1856–1960)
The playwright won the Nobel Prize for Literature in 1925 and was 82 when he won the Best Screenplay Oscar for *Pygmalion* (1938) – the only person ever to win both awards.

3 ## Winston Churchill (1874–1965)
Begun in 1937 but delayed by the Second World War and his prime ministership, Churchill finished writing his *History of the English-Speaking Peoples* when he reached the age of 83.

4 ## William Gladstone (1809–98)
Gladstone retired as prime minister in 1894, at the age of 84.

5 ## Doris Lessing (b. 1919)
At the age of 88, Lessing (born in Persia to British parents) became the oldest British Nobel Prize-winner in 2007.

6 ## P. G. Wodehouse (1881–1975)
His novel *Aunts Aren't Gentlemen* was published on 17 October 1974, two days after the author's 93rd birthday.

7 ## Margaret Murray (1863–1963)
Murray, an anthropologist and specialist on witchcraft and Egyptian mummies, published her autobiography, *My First Hundred Years*, in 1963. She died soon afterwards.

8 ## Robert Mayer (1879–1985)
German-born philanthropist (a British citizen from 1902) and founder of the Robert Mayer concerts for young people, Mayer became the oldest Briton to be knighted, on his 100th birthday. Like Murray, he wrote a centenary autobiography, *My First 100 Years* (1979), dying at the age of 106.

9 ## Eluned (b. 1903) and William Jones (b. 1901)
Britain's oldest married couple celebrated their 84th anniversary on 3 February 2007, when she was 103 and he 105.

10 ## Mary Davies Wilburn (1883–1987)
Wilburn was the oldest survivor of the *Titanic* – the ship went down in 1912, when she was 28, and she lived until she was 104.

ONE-EYED BRITONS

1   **Elizabeth Blackwell (1821–1910)**
A pioneer doctor and women's rights activist, Blackwell was prevented from becoming a surgeon by the loss of sight in one eye.

2   **Gordon Brown (b. 1951)**
The British prime minister was left blind in his left eye as a result of a childhood rugby accident.

3   **Joe Davis (1901–78)**
Despite being almost blind in his right eye, Davis became a professional snooker player and was world champion in 1927–40 and 1946.

4   **George Frideric Handel (1685–1759)**
The German-born (but from 1727 British) composer started turning blind in 1751, becoming completely blind in one eye.

5   **Rex Harrison (1908–90)**
As a result of childhood measles, the British actor best known for his role of Henry Higgins in *My Fair Lady* had little sight in his left eye.

6   **Eric Hosking (1909–91)**
A photographer specializing in birds, Hosking lost his left eye in 1937 when he was attacked by a tawny owl. His autobiography was titled *An Eye for a Bird*.

7   **Samuel Johnson (1709–84)**
Although almost blind in his left eye and with weak vision in his right, Johnson managed to compile the great dictionary that bears his name.

8   **Horatio Nelson (1758–1805)**
Naval hero Nelson's right eye was injured by stones from a cannon blast during the siege of Calvi, Corsica, on 12 July 1794. He did not, as some portraits suggest, wear an eye patch.

9   **Peter Sutcliffe (b. 1946)**
The so-called Yorkshire Ripper was attacked by another inmate in Broadmoor Prison on 10 March 1997, losing the sight of his left eye.

10   **Archibald Wavell (1883–1950)**
The British military commander and Viceroy of India (1943–7) lost his left eye on 16 June 1915, during the Second Battle of Ypres.

BRITISH SAINTS

1   **St David (*c*.500–589)**
A monastic teacher and, since the 12th century, patron saint of Wales, he was buried in St David's Cathedral, Pembrokeshire.

2   **St Cuthbert (*c*.634–687)**
At the death of Cuthbert, Bishop of Lindisfarne, a cult arose around his remains and Durham Cathedral was established on the site of his last resting place.

3   **St Bede (*c*.672–735)**
A Northumbrian monk and the first English historian, he wrote *The Ecclesiastical History of the English People*. Known as 'The Venerable Bede', he was canonized in 1899.

4   **St Columba (521–597)**
Irish-born Columba founded a monastery on the Scottish island of Iona, from which much of Scotland was converted to Christianity.

5   **St Alban (3rd century)**
The first British Christian martyr, he was said to have been beheaded at Verulamium, renamed St Alban's after him.

6   **St Thomas More (1478–1535)**
Formerly Henry VIII's Lord Chancellor, he was executed after opposing the king over his divorce from Anne Boleyn. Along with John Fisher, he was canonized in 1935.

7   **St Swithun (*c*.800–863)**
Swithun was the Bishop of Winchester, where he was buried. It was believed that if it rained on his feast day, it foretold rain for the next 40 days.

8   **St Edmund Campion (1540–81)**
Tried as a traitor under Queen Elizabeth I, he was tortured, hanged, drawn and quartered at Tyburn. He was canonized in 1970 as one of the 'Forty Martyrs of England and Wales'.

9   **St Edmund (841–869)**
The king of East Anglia was martyred, according to legend, by being shot with arrows and beheaded. His tomb at Bury St Edmunds became a popular shrine in the Middle Ages.

10   **St Thomas Becket (*c*.1118–70)**
The Archbishop of Canterbury was supposedly murdered on the orders of Henry II. He was canonized three years after his death.

10

BUILDINGS DESIGNED
by Sir Christopher Wren

1 ### The Monument, London
Completed in 1676, the column commemorates the Great Fire of London of 1666. Its height of 61 m (202 ft) is equal to the distance to the baker's shop where the fire broke out.

2 ### Wren Library, Cambridge
The library at Trinity College was completed in 1695 and later named after the architect.

3 ### St Paul's Cathedral, London
Wren's greatest work replaced 'Old St Paul's', the medieval cathedral destroyed in the Great Fire of London.

4 ### Royal Hospital, Chelsea, London
Built to house injured soldiers, this was based on the design of the Hôpital des Invalides, Paris. It was completed by 1692.

5 ### Royal Observatory, Greenwich, London
Flamsteed House, Britain's first scientific research building, was built in 1675–6. With architect Nicholas Hawksmoor, Wren also designed the nearby Greenwich Hospital.

6 ### Temple Bar, London
Marking the west entrance to the City of London, Temple Bar was damaged in the Great Fire. Wren's construction, which replaced it, was used to display the heads of traitors.

7 ### St Clement Danes, London
Wren's church, which replaced the previous medieval structure in 1682, was damaged during the Blitz in 1941, but was rebuilt and dedicated to the Royal Air Force.

8 ### St Mary-le-Bow, London
Like St Paul's, this church replaced one destroyed during the Great Fire, its steeple being completed in 1680. By tradition, to be a true Cockney one must be born within the sound of Bow Bells.

9 ### Christ Church, Oxford
Tom Tower (named after the bell it houses), the entrance to Christ Church College, was designed by Wren and completed in 1682.

10 ### St Bride's, London
Designed by Wren in 1672, its multi-tiered spire, a later addition, is said to have inspired the traditional British wedding cake.

GREAT SURVIVING STRUCTURES
by Isambard Kingdom Brunel

1 **Wharncliffe Viaduct, May 1837**
The 270-m (886-ft) eight-arched brick railway viaduct between Hanwell and Ealing was Brunel's first major project and the first viaduct with an electric telegraph (1839).

2 **Maidenhead Railway Bridge, 31 May 1838**
The world's flattest and widest brick arch bridge when it was built, this is depicted in Turner's painting *Rain, Steam and Speed* (1844).

3 **Bristol Temple Meads Station, 31 Aug 1840**
At the time it was opened, Bristol Temple Meads was the largest single-span building ever constructed.

4 **Box Tunnel, 30 Jun 1841**
On the Great Western Railway line between Bath and Chippenham, the 2,937-m (1-mile, 1,422-yard) tunnel was at the time the world's longest rail tunnel.

5 **Thames Tunnel, 25 Mar 1843**
Built in 1825–43, the first tunnel under the Thames was originally used by pedestrians but was converted to a rail link in 1869 and is currently being extensively refurbished.

6 **SS *Great Britain*, 19 Jul 1843**
Launched in Bristol in 1843, the 98-m (322-ft) steamship was the first iron-hulled trans-atlantic liner. Abandoned in the Falkland Islands, she was rescued in 1970 and returned to dry dock in Bristol, where she has been extensively restored.

7 **Hungerford Bridge, 1 May 1845**
Brunel's original 433-m (1,462-ft) Thames footbridge was rebuilt as a rail bridge after his death, its cables incorporated in his Clifton Suspension Bridge.

8 **Paddington Station, 29 May 1854**
Although modified, much of Brunel's original building has survived. A statue of him was unveiled here in 1982.

9 **Royal Albert Bridge, 2 May 1859**
Crossing the Tamar between Plymouth and Saltash, the bridge was opened by Prince Albert on 2 May 1859. Brunel died soon after its completion.

10 **Clifton Suspension Bridge, 8 Dec 1864**
Brunel's design for a bridge spanning the Avon in Bristol was chosen after he won a competition in 1831, but it was not completed until five years after his death.

FIRST BOOKS
by Beatrix Potter

	Book	Year
1	*The Tale of Peter Rabbit*	1902
2	*The Tale of Squirrel Nutkin*	1903
3	*The Tailor of Gloucester*	1903
4	*The Tale of Benjamin Bunny*	1904
5	*The Tale of Two Bad Mice*	1904
6	*The Tale of Mrs Tiggy-Winkle*	1905
7	*The Tale of the Pie and the Patty-Pan*	1905
8	*The Tale of Mr Jeremy Fisher*	1906
9	*The Story of a Fierce Bad Rabbit*	1906
10	*The Story of Miss Moppet*	1906

Beatrix Potter (1866–1943) wrote and illustrated *The Tale of Peter Rabbit* and attempted to interest publishers in it, without success. She published 250 copies herself, followed by a further 200. Frederick Warne then acquired rights and published the first edition on 2 October 1902 – since when it has sold over 40 million copies. Beatrix Potter followed it up with one or more books a year for the next 10 years, then with less frequency, creating a total of 24 books in her lifetime.

FIRST NOVELS
by Charles Dickens

	Novel	Serial	Book
1	*The Pickwick Papers*	Mar 1836–Oct 1837	17 Nov 1837
2	*The Adventures of Oliver Twist*	Feb 1837–Apr 1839	9 Nov 1838
3	*The Life and Adventures of Nicholas Nickleby*	Mar 1838–Sep 1839	23 Oct 1839
4=	*The Old Curiosity Shop*	Apr 1840–Feb 1841	15 Dec 1841
=	*Barnaby Rudge*	Feb–Nov 1841	15 Dec 1841
6	*The Life and Adventures of Martin Chuzzlewit*	Jan 1843–Jul 1844	16 Jul 1844
7	*Dombey and Son*	Oct 1846–Apr 1848	12 Apr 1848
8	*David Copperfield*	May 1849–Nov 1850	14 Nov 1850
9	*Bleak House*	Mar 1852–Sep 1853	12 Sep 1853
10	*Hard Times*	Apr–Aug 1854	7 Aug 1854

Dickens's novels were serialized in monthly magazines before being published as books, with readers anxiously awaiting the appearance of each new episode. As well as these full-length novels, *A Christmas Carol* and four other short 'Christmas Books' were published annually from 1843 to 1848.

TOP 10

MOST EXPENSIVE PAINTINGS
by British artists

	Painting/artist*/auction	Price
1	*Triptych*, Francis Bacon (Irish-born), Sotheby's, New York, 14 May 2008	£44,231,469
2	*Giudecca, La Donna della Salute and San Giorgio*, J. M. W. Turner, Christie's, New York, 6 Apr 2006	£20,439,038
3	*Benefits Supervisor Sleeping*, Lucian Freud, Christie's, New York, 13 May 2008	£17,218,418
4	*Group with Parasols*, John Singer Sargent (US-born), Sotheby's, New York, 1 Dec 2004	£12,311,879
5	*The Lock*, John Constable, Sotheby's, London, 14 Nov 1990	£10,780,000
6	*Portrait of Omai*, Sir Joshua Reynolds, Sotheby's, London, 29 Nov 2001	£10,343,500
7	*St Cecilia*, John William Waterhouse, Christie's, London, 14 Jun 2000	£6,603,750
8	*Eternity*, Damien Hirst, Phillips de Pury, London, 13 Oct 2007	£4,724,000
9	*Good Friday, Daisy Nook*, L. S. Lowry, Christie's, London, 8 Jun 2007	£3,772,000
10	*Portrait of the Royal Tiger*, George Stubbs, Christie's, London, 8 Jun 1995	£3,191,500

* Limited to the most expensive work by each artist

MOST EXPENSIVE PAINTINGS
by J. M. W. Turner

	Painting/auction	Price
1	*Giudecca, La Donna della Salute and San Giorgio*, Christie's, New York, 6 Apr 2006	£20,439,038
2	*Seascape, Folkestone*, Sotheby's, London, 5 Jul 1984	£6,700,000
3	*The Blue Rigi: Lake of Lucerne, sunrise*, Christie's, London, 5 Jun 2006	£5,832,000
4	*Pope's Villa at Twickenham*, Sotheby's, London, 9 Jul 2008	£5,417,250
5	*A Swiss Lake, Lungernzee*, Sotheby's, London, 4 Jul 2007	£3,604,000
6	*Glaucus and Scylla*, Christie's, New York, 19 Apr 2007	£3,200,191
7	*Juliet and her Nurse*, Sotheby's, New York, 29 May 1980	£3,128,884
8	*Venice: Looking towards the Dogana and San Giorgio Maggiore, with a storm approaching*, Sotheby's, London, 4 Jul 2007	£2,988,000
9	*Bamborough Castle*, Sotheby's, London, 5 Dec 2007	£2,932,500
10	*Fort Vimieux*, Sotheby's, London, 1 Jul 2004	£2,469,600

Although since overtaken by a substantial margin, in 1980 Joseph Mallord William Turner's *Juliet and her Nurse* held the world record for the most expensive painting ever sold at auction. Four years later, his work *Seascape, Folkestone*, established a new record.

FINAL RESTING PLACES
of the ashes of famous Britons

1 **H(enry) Rider Haggard**
The author of *King Solomon's Mines* died in London on 14 May 1925. His ashes were buried in Ditchingham Church, Norfolk.

2 **Thomas Hardy**
The author of *Tess of the D'Urbervilles* died on 11 January 1928. His ashes were buried in Westminster Abbey (the rule since 1907, when philanthropist Angela Burdett-Coutts body was the last body to be buried there, other than that of the unknown warrior in 1920). Hardy's heart was separately buried in Stinsford, Dorset. An unproven rumour that a cat ate the heart and that an empty box (or possibly the cat itself) was buried has circulated ever since.

3 **John Buchan**
The author of *The Thirty-Nine Steps* and Governor-General of Canada died in Canada on 11 February 1940 and was cremated in Montreal. His ashes were returned to England and buried in the churchyard of St Thomas, Elsfield, Oxfordshire.

4 **Virginia Woolf**
After the author drowned herself in the River Ouse near Lewes, East Sussex, on 28 March 1941, her ashes were buried beneath an elm tree in the garden of her home, Monk's House. Her husband, Leonard Woolf, died at the house on 14 August 1969 and his ashes were also buried there.

5 **Beatrix Potter**
The *Peter Rabbit* author and illustrator died on 22 December 1943. She was cremated in Blackpool and her ashes scattered on her sheep farm at Monk Coniston in the Lake District.

6 **George Bernard Shaw**
The playwright died on 2 November 1950. His ashes were mixed with those of his wife, Charlotte, who had died in 1943, and were scattered in the flowerbeds of their garden at Ayot St Lawrence, Hertfordshire.

7 **Tony Hancock**
The comedian committed suicide in Sydney, Australia, on 24 June 1968. His body was cremated and the ashes brought to England by satirist Willie Rushton (who denied the rumour that they were tasted by a customs officer who suspected the grey powder was drugs), to be buried at St Dunstan's Church, Cranford Park, London.

8   Aldous Huxley

The British author died on the same day as President Kennedy's assassination, 22 November 1963, and so received little publicity. His body was cremated in Los Angeles and his ashes returned to England for burial in his parents' grave at Compton, Surrey.

9   Sir Laurence Olivier

After the actor's death on 11 July 1989, his ashes were buried in Westminster Abbey – the fifth actor so honoured, after David Garrick, Ben Jonson, Anne Bracegirdle and Thomas Betterton.

10   Sir Stanley Matthews

The footballer died on 23 February 2000, his ashes being buried beneath the pitch of Stoke City's Britannia Stadium.

As early as 1769 Honoretta Pratt was illegally cremated in an open grave in St George's, Hanover Square, London, but it was over a century until the notion of cremation was revived when, in 1874, Queen Victoria's surgeon Sir Henry Thompson founded the Cremation Society of England, along with such luminaries as the Pre-Raphaelite painter John Millais, *Alice in Wonderland* illustrator John Tenniel and novelist Anthony Trollope. The first crematorium was opened in Woking, Surrey, in 1878 and on 17 March 1879 tested by cremating a horse. The legality of cremation remained in question until 1884, when eccentric Welsh doctor William Price attempted to cremate the body of his infant son, Jesus Christ, for which he was tried but acquitted. Britain's first cremation, of Jeanette Pickersgill, took place on 26 March 1885. Today, over 70 per cent of bodies are disposed of by cremation in Britain, placing the country fourth in the world after China, Japan and the USA. Ashes are kept in urns, buried or scattered, fired skywards in rockets or utilized creatively, as in the case of D. H. Lawrence, whose remains were mixed with concrete to create a permanent shrine at his former home in Taos, New Mexico.

10

BRITONS' FAMOUS LAST WORDS*

1   'All my possessions for a moment of time.'
    Elizabeth I, 1603

2   'It's all been very interesting.'
    Traveller Lady Mary Wortley Montagu, 1762

3   'Die, my dear doctor? That's the last thing I shall do.'
    Viscount Palmerston, British prime minister, 1865

4   'I am not the least afraid to die.'
    Charles Darwin, author of *On the Origin of Species*, 1882

5   'Oh, that peace may come ... Bertie!'
    Queen Victoria, 1901 (the references are to the war in progress in South Africa and her late
    husband, Prince Albert)

6   'Bugger Bognor!'
    George V, on being told he might go there to recuperate, 1936

7   'Go away. I'm all right.'
    H. G. Wells, author of *The Time Machine*, 1946

8   'Am I dying or is this my birthday?'
    Nancy Astor, Britain's first female MP to take her seat, 1964

9   'I'm bored with it all.'
    Sir Winston Churchill, 1965

10 'My God! What's happened?'
    Diana, Princess of Wales, 1997

    * According to contemporary reports or popular belief

HISTORIC
BRITAIN

BRITISH WORLD FIRSTS

	Invention	Inventor	Date
1	Vaccination	Edward Jenner (1749–1823)	1796
2	Raincoat (GB patent 4804)	Charles Macintosh (1766–1843)	1823
3	Postage stamp	Rowland Hill (1795–1879)	1840
4	Christmas card	John Calcott Horsley (1817–1903)	1843
5	Anaesthetic (chloroform)	James Young Simpson (1811–70)	1847
6	Vacuum cleaner (GB patent 17,433)	Hubert Cecil Booth (1871–1955)	1901
7	Penicillin	Alexander Fleming (1881–1955)	1928
8	Hovercraft (GB patent 854,211)	Christopher Cockerell (1910–99)	1955
9	Test-tube baby	Patrick Christopher Steptoe (1913–88)	1978
10	World Wide Web	Tim Berners-Lee (b. 1955)	1991

KEY EVENTS
in British history

1   Roman conquest, AD 43
    The invasion under Emperor Claudius in the summer of AD 43, with an army of some
    20,000, established Roman rule that was to last for almost 400 years.

2   Norman Conquest, 1066
    William of Normandy and an 8,400-strong army defeated and killed King Harold at the
    decisive Battle of Hastings on 14 October 1066.

3   Sealing of the Magna Carta, 1215
    King John's sealing of the Magna Carta at Runnymede on 15 June 1215 codified rights such
    as *habeas corpus* and limited the power of the king.

4   Britain's first printing press, 1476
    Having printed the first book in English in Bruges in 1474, William Caxton set up Britain's
    first printing press in Westminster three years later.

5   Defeat of the Spanish Armada, 1588
    The invasion of Britain by Spain ended in disaster on 8 August 1588 when a combination
    of attack by the British and storms destroyed the Spanish fleet.

6   Publication of the King James Bible, 1611
    Although not the first English translation of the Bible, the authorized version reflected the
    doctrine of the Church of England and is considered a literary masterpiece.

7   Execution of Charles I, 1649
    King Charles I was captured, tried and, on 30 January 1649, executed in London.
    Cromwell's parliament and its successors ruled England until the Restoration in 1660.

8   Act of Union, 1707
    The Act of Union that came into effect on 1 May 1707 united England and Scotland into
    the United Kingdom of Great Britain.

9   Battle of Trafalgar, 1805
    The battle between the British and the French at Trafalgar on 21 October 1805 resulted in
    the death of Admiral Lord Nelson but was a significant naval victory for the British.

10 Battle of Britain, 1940
    The decisive period of air warfare between the RAF and German Luftwaffe, from 10 July to
    31 October 1940, was named the Battle of Britain in a speech by Winston Churchill on
    18 June 1940.

10 OF THE WORST TIMES TO HAVE LIVED in Britain

1   **793**
    On 8 June Vikings made their first attack on England, sacking the monastery at Lindisfarne, Northumberland. This marks the beginning of the Viking age, when much of the country was ravaged by invaders.

2   **1348–49**
    The Black Death arrived in Britain via ships landing at Bristol in the summer of 1348. By May of the following year 30–40 per cent of the population – as much as 80–90 per cent in certain villages – some 800,000 to 1,500,000, were dead. Outbreaks continued at intervals for the rest of the century.

3   **1665–66**
    The Great Plague wiped out a large proportion of London's inhabitants, variously estimated at between 10,000 and 100,000, perhaps as much as one-fifth of the population. By the time of the Great Fire of London (2–3 September 1666), which killed few people, it was already waning.

4   **1703**
    The Great Storm of 24 November–2 December 1703 was probably the worst ever to affect Britain. Trees were uprooted, buildings destroyed, flooding occurred and many ships, including Royal Navy vessels, were lost. Among the 8,000–15,000 dead were Richard Kidder, the Bishop of Bath and Wells, and his wife, Elizabeth, killed when a chimney fell through the roof onto their bed.

5   **1740**
    In the coldest winter to strike Britain since records began, many died of cold or during the famine and drought that followed. Icebergs appeared in the English Channel, water transport was halted and watermills and wells froze, with the result that coal became scarce and food prices rose rapidly. A 'Frost Fair' was held on the frozen Thames on which the ice was so thick that a whole ox was roasted.

6   **1845–49**
    Ireland, at this time part of Britain, suffered its devastating potato famine – a blight that destroyed the country's staple crop – with an estimated million people dying. Many emigrated to the USA and other countries.

7   1849

Following a cholera epidemic in 1832, another struck with as many as 12,847 Londoners dying in the last three months of the year, along with 5,308 in Liverpool, 1,834 in Hull and many elsewhere. It was not until 1854 that Dr John Snow discovered the link between a cholera outbreak in Soho, London, and the water supply.

8   1858

Known as the year of the 'Great Stink', when sewage draining into the Thames, combined with a hot summer, made the river unapproachable. Many riverside buildings, including the House of Commons, were virtually uninhabitable. This was the final spur to the major improvement of London's sewers in the 1860s, masterminded by engineer Joseph Bazalgette.

9   1918

During the final months of the First World War, Britain was hit by an influenza pandemic in which some 225,000 died. It began in March 1918 and spread rapidly as a result of post-war movements of troops and refugees.

10   1940–41

The period from 7 September 1940 to 10 May 1941 was the period of the Blitz, when an estimated 18,800 tons of bombs rained down on London. Some 1,436 people were killed on the night of 10–11 May 1941 alone, and even people sheltering in Underground stations previously believed to be safe were killed when Marble Arch, Balham and Bank received direct hits. In all, some 43,000 died.

BRITISH TIME CAPSULES

1   Embankment, London
Two earthenware jars installed under Cleopatra's Needle on London's Embankment in 1878 are the UK's earliest time capsule, though no opening date was scheduled. Its contents include copies of *Whitaker's Almanack*, *Bradshaw's Railway Guide*, Bibles in various languages, British newspapers, a complete set of British currency and one Indian rupee (Queen Victoria had been proclaimed Empress of India two years earlier), a box of cigars, hairpins, a razor, a baby's feeding bottle, toys and portraits of Queen Victoria and 12 of Britain's prettiest women. A range of artefacts relate to the Needle itself and its journey from Egypt, including copies of *Engineering* magazine in which the achievement is described, iron ropes and submarine cables, a bronze half-inch to a foot scale model of the obelisk and a piece of granite chipped from it, a parchment copy of Samuel Birch's translation of the Needle's hieroglyphics, a two-foot ruler, a map of London and a Tangye's hydraulic jack, as used to erect the Needle.

2   Blackpool Tower
A time capsule was placed beneath the foundation stone on 29 September 1891, with a recording of the builder's voice, newspapers and other artefacts. It could not be found when building work was carried out on the Tower, showing how important it is not only to ensure that the capsule is preserved, but also that a careful record of its exact location is safely kept.

3   London University
Time capsules were originally inspired by ritualized foundation-stone deposits, a continuing practice. Dignitaries place current coins, newspapers and sometimes other low-value items during early construction work, which may then only be retrieved on demolition, but beneath Senate House in central London lies a rare, priceless, unstealable 1933 penny. (Only seven examples of this numismatic treasure are known to exist – one other was preserved with other coins of the year in a time capsule in the cornerstone of St Cross Church, Middleton, Yorkshire, but was stolen in 1970; to prevent a repeat of this theft, one beneath the foundation stone of St Mary's Church, Kirkstall, Leeds, was removed by the church and sold at auction in 1972.)

4   Television Centre, London
The long-running BBC TV programme *Blue Peter* stuffed a box with viewers' suggestions – which included a copy of the 1970 *Blue Peter* annual, a set of decimal coins, introduced in 1971, and photographs of the three presenters – and buried it at Television Centre on 7 June 1971. The box was relocated in 1984 and buried unopened alongside another box containing hairs from Goldie the *Blue Peter* labrador, a record of the programme's theme tune arranged by Mike Oldfield and video footage of the moving of the dog Petra's statue. The original capsule was finally reopened as intended in 2000. The *Blue Peter* Millennium

Time Capsule was buried beneath the Millennium Dome on 11 June 1998, containing a *Blue Peter* badge and history of the programme, a set of Teletubby dolls, an insulin pen and a France '98 football. The capsule is scheduled to be opened in 2050.

5 Castle Howard, Yorkshire

The container buried by the BBC in 1982, inspired by Japan's 5,000-year Expo '70 time capsule, is addressed more modestly to the year 3982. Compilers worried whether including differently scaled models would confuse finders of the future: the double-decker bus was smaller than the Rolls-Royce.

6 Clatterbridge Hospital, Merseyside

Comedian Ken Dodd's pink 'tickling stick', a Rubik's cube and a Royal Wedding crown accompanied more sombre contents of a cyclotron buried as a time capsule here in 1981. Other items included a set of old radium needles and part of a computer used in cancer treatment.

7 Kew Gardens, Surrey

In 1985, for the World Wildlife Fund Plant Campaign, broadcaster David Attenborough buried a 'botanical ark' here. Sealed in a glass ball were 10 seeds of basic crops and endangered species. Addressed to 2985, this was mainly a plea to the present to tackle environmental change.

8 Royal Garden Hotel, London

In 1986, the late royal photographer Patrick Lichfield buried a time capsule addressed to the year 2011 at this Kensington hotel on the occasion of its 20th anniversary. In 1996, another was added and both were readdressed to 2015.

9 Globe Theatre, London

Time capsules were awarded as incentives to schools fundraising for the new Globe Theatre, which opened in 1997 on London's Bankside. Public figures burying them in the basement as construction work progressed included Prince Edward (1992), a descendant of the Bard Sir William Shakespeare (1993) and actress Zoë Wanamaker (1994).

10 Guildford Castle, Surrey

In 2000, the 100-m³ (3,531-ft³) Millennium Vault in the side of a hill in the castle's grounds qualified as the UK's biggest time capsule. Items sealed inside for 1,000 years include life-size photos of singer Dame Vera Lynn, a conserved Mini car, trainers and a violin.

Source: Brian Durrans, International Time Capsule Society

BRITISH EVENTS THAT OCCURRED ON Friday the 13th

1   **Friday, 13 October 1066**
This was the last day England was under Anglo-Saxon rule. Fresh from his victory at Stamford Bridge, Yorkshire, where on 25 September he had defeated the Viking force of Harald Hardrada, King Harold II arrived at Senlac Hill with his army of 7,500. In the Battle of Hastings the following day, Harold was killed and William the Conqueror became king, so beginning Norman rule of England.

2   **Friday, 13 December 1867**
A failed attempt to free Fenian (Irish nationalist) prisoner Richard O'Sullivan-Burke from Coldbath Fields Prison, Clerkenwell, London, by blowing up the wall destroyed a row of nearby houses, leaving 12 dead and 120 injured. The following year Michael Barrett, one of those found guilty of the bombing, became the last person in Britain to be publicly executed when he was hanged outside Newgate Prison.

3   **Friday, 13 February 1891**
Although the murders believed to have been perpetrated by Jack the Ripper took place in 1888, Frances Coles, killed in Whitechapel, has been claimed to have been his final victim. Her body was found by police constable Ernest Thompson in Swallow Gardens at 2.20 a.m. The police, fearing a revival of the Ripper fear that had gripped London three years earlier, conducted a thorough investigation and arrested James Sadler, a ship's fireman. He was exonerated at Coles's inquest and the crime remained unsolved.

4   **Friday, 13 October 1905**
Sir Henry Irving, the first British actor to be awarded a knighthood, gave his last perform-ance in the title role in Alfred, Lord Tennyson's play *Becket*, on stage in Bradford. Soon afterwards, he collapsed in the lobby of the Midland Hotel, dying in the arms of his dresser, Walter Collinson. A week later his funeral took place at Westminster Abbey.

5   **Friday, 13 August 1915**
George Joseph Smith, the infamous 'Brides in the Bath' murderer, was hanged by John Ellis at Maidstone prison. Although already married, under the pretext of being a travelling antique dealer, Smith 'married' three women, Beatrice Mundy, Alice Burnham and Margaret Lofty in different parts of Britain and murdered them by drowning them in their baths to gain their fortunes or claim on life assurance policies.

6   **Friday, 13 June 1930**
Sir Henry Segrave, British record-breaker, was killed, along with his mechanic Vic Halliwell, in a speedboat crash on Lake Windermere after he had set a new world record for the mile of 158.93 km/h (98.76 mph) in his boat *Miss England II*. Previously, in 1927, Segrave had been the first person to drive a car at over 200 mph.

7   Friday, 13 October 1939

During the night, German U-boat *U-47*, captained by Günther Prien, entered Scapa Flow, Orkney, and torpedoed British battleship HMS *Royal Oak* at anchor. She sank the following day with the loss of 833 lives, the first major marine victim of Second World War. The wreck is a designated war grave.

8   Friday, 13 December 1940

During an air raid on Sheffield, many people took shelter in the cellars of Marples Hotel, which received a direct hit, killing some 70. Although trapped beneath the rubble, several people escaped unscathed, while billiards champion Joe Davis, who was booked to play at the hotel that night, was unable to make the journey from Hull as a result of bomb damage to the railway network.

9   Friday, 13 January 1984

B2, one of the eight huge cooling towers at Fiddlers Ferry Power Station, Lancashire, collapsed in a high wind. A study of the effect of wind turbulence on closely grouped towers was launched to ensure that such events do not recur.

10   Friday, 13 November 1987

At Bristol Crown Court, DNA evidence from a rape case was used to convict a criminal for the first time in Britain, as a result of which Robert Melias was sentenced to eight years imprisonment. Since this landmark case, techniques have been refined and DNA profiling is now a major element in identifying individuals and securing convictions.

Triskaidekaphobia – the fear of the number 13 – has been explained as relating to the number present at the Last Supper, but it is present in many cultures, including some that predate Christianity. The superstition means, for example, that many buildings do not have a 13th floor, while ships are rarely launched on the 13th of any month, especially a Friday the 13th (fear of which is known as paraskavedekatriaphobia), which is thought to be particularly unlucky; in Christian tradition this may be because the Crucifixion took place on a Friday, while the number 13 figures in various British superstitions and traditions – the hangman's noose has 13 twists and there are 13 steps to the gallows. There can be as many as three Friday the 13ths in any year – as in 2009 – while the longest possible period without a Friday the 13th in the calendar is 14 months. Recent statistical research has shown that Friday the 13th is not notably unlucky – in fact, fewer accidents are reported, perhaps because people are taking extra care on these 'unlucky' days.

DEFUNCT BRITISH HOLIDAYS

1   Handsel Monday
    The first Monday of the year, a day when gifts were offered, now replaced by Boxing Day.

2   Plough Monday
    The first Monday after Twelfth Night, marking the end of the Christmas period, when a plough festival was held in rural areas, with ploughboys collecting 'plough-money' for a riotous celebration.

3   Merry Monday
    Once spent in debauched revelry, Merry Monday is the day before Shrove Tuesday (which can fall from 3 February to 9 March).

4   St George's Day
    23 April, once a national holiday in honour of the patron saint of England.

5   Empire Day
    Established after the South African War and held on Queen Victoria's birthday, 24 May, it was replaced by Commonwealth Day in 1958.

6   Oak Apple Day
    Also called Royal Oak Day, 29 May, the birthday of Charles II (who is said to have hidden in an oak tree after his defeat at Worcester) and the day he entered London at the 1660 Restoration of the monarchy. It was officially abolished in 1859.

7   Lammas Day
    Celebrated on 1 August, a Quarter Day between Midsummer and Michaelmas, in Anglo-Saxon England the time of a 'feast of first fruits' from the harvest.

8   Michaelmas
    The festival of St Michael and All Angels, celebrated on 29 September.

9   Trafalgar Day
    The commemoration of the British victory at the Battle of Trafalgar on 21 October 1805 was celebrated throughout the 19th century, but declined during the 20th.

10 Martinmas
    The feast day of St Martin on 11 November, once the occasion of hiring fairs.

LANDOWNERS IN BRITAIN
1872–2001

	1872 Landowner/acres	2001 Landowner/acres
1	Duke of Sutherland (1,358,545)	Duke of Buccleuch and Queensberry (270,700)
2	Duke of Buccleuch and Queensberry (460,108)	Dukedom of Atholl (Trustees) (148,000)
3	Earl of Breadalbane (438,358)	Prince of Wales (141,000)
4	Lady Matheson (424,560)	Duke of Northumberland (132,200)
5	Sir Charles Ross (356,500)	Duke of Westminster (129,300)
6	Earl of Seafield (305,930)	Capt. Alwyne Farquharson (106,500)
7	Duke of Richmond and Gordon (286,411)	Earl of Seafield (101,000)
8	Earl of Fife (249,220)	Viscount Cowdray (93,600)
9	Sir Alexander Matheson (220,663)	Robert Fleming (88,900)
10	Duke of Atholl (201,640)	Edmund Vesty (86,300)

Source: Kevin Cahill, *Who Owns Britain*, 2001

KNIGHTS OF THE ROUND TABLE

1 Sir Bedivere
The legend of King Arthur and the Knights of the Round Table describes him as one-handed, but a skilled warrior. On Arthur's death, he is the knight who returns the sword Excalibur to the Lady of the Lake.

2 Sir Bors
Sir Bors the Younger (the son of a king of the same name), he is one of the knights who find the Holy Grail, eventually dying on a crusade.

3 Sir Caradoc
One of King Arthur's closest aides, he is said to be the son of Eliavres the wizard and the founder of the kingdom of Gwent.

4 Sir Galahad
The son of Sir Lancelot and Elaine of Carbonek, he is a prominent figure in the Arthurian legend and accompanies the king on his quest for the Holy Grail.

5 Sir Gawain
The son of King Lot and nephew of King Arthur, he is the central character in the legend of Sir Gawain and the Green Knight.

6 Sir Kay
Arthur's foster-brother and one of the first Knights of the Round Table, he figures as a leading character in T. H. White's novel *The Sword in the Stone* and its sequels.

7 Sir Lancelot
Originally Arthur's closet companion, Lancelot is noted for his affair with Arthur's queen Guinevere and for his role in their Holy Grail quest.

8 Sir Percival
One of the Grail-seekers, Sir Percival is the *Parsifal* of Richard Wagner's opera.

9 Sir Sagramore
The son of the king of Hungary, he travels to England to become a Knight of the Round Table.

10 Sir Tristan
The legend of Tristan and Iseult (or Isolde) of Ireland recounts the story of their romance.

BRITISH SPIES

1   Christopher Marlowe (1564–93)
Marlowe was recruited as a spy by Elizabeth I's spymaster Francis Walsingham. His murder by stabbing in a brawl has been claimed to have been connected with his espionage work.

2   Daniel Defoe (1660–1731)
The author of *Robinson Crusoe* was also an agent in the service of Queen Anne who travelled the country under assumed names, seeking evidence of Jacobite plots against the Crown.

3   George Lockhart (1673–1731)
After being imprisoned in Edinburgh Castle following the rising of 1715, Lockhart became a Jacobite spy for the Pretender Charles Stuart until his death in a duel.

4   James Robertson (1758–1820)
Robertson was a Benedictine monk known as Gallus who, in 1808, posing as a cigar merchant, travelled to Europe to spy for Britain against Napoleon.

5   Robert Baden-Powell (1857–1941)
Baden-Powell's fame rests on his founding of the Boy Scout movement, but prior to that he operated as a British spy in South Africa, North Africa and Europe.

6   Anthony Blunt (1907–83)
Art historian and Surveyor of the King's (later Queen's) Pictures, Blunt spied for the Soviet Union. His activities were made public in 1979 and he was stripped of his knighthood.

7   Guy Burgess (1911–63)
Double-agent Burgess was a British government employee who spied for the Soviet Union. He fled to Moscow in 1951 and died there.

8   Kim Philby (1912–88)
Philby was an MI6 officer and member of the so-called 'Cambridge Five', recruited in 1933, who in 1963 fled to the Soviet Union.

9   Donald Maclean (1913–83)
While at Cambridge University in the 1930s, Maclean was recruited as a Soviet agent by Anthony Blunt. He worked in the British Embassy in Washington, DC, but when suspicions were aroused he and Burgess fled to Moscow where he died.

10   George Blake (b. 1922)
Double-agent Blake was exposed and jailed for a record 42 years, but escaped from Wormwood Scrubs prison in 1966 and has lived in Moscow ever since.

BRITISH HIGHWAYMEN

1   John Clavell (1601–43)
John Clavell was a member of an old Dorsetshire family, the heir to his uncle, Sir William Clavell, whom he later admitted he had 'grossly injured' by becoming a highwayman 'out of great necessity'. After being dismissed from Oxford University for stealing valuables from his college and committing a number of robberies at Gad's Hill, Kent, and elsewhere, he was arrested. In prison he wrote *A Recantation of an Ill-Led Life*, a grovelling apology that achieved its desired effect: he received a royal pardon from Charles I and was released, but was disinherited and became a playwright, lawyer and quack doctor.

2   James Hind (*c*.1616-52)
'Captain' James Hind was a notorious Royalist highwayman from Chipping Norton, Oxfordshire. While imprisoned in London, he met Thomas Allen, a highwayman with whom he joined forces on their release. A number of pamphlets celebrated his exploits, one claiming that he served in the army in Ireland; on his return to England, he was arrested, tried for treason and hanged, drawn and quartered at Worcester.

3   John Cottington (*c*.1614–59)
John Cottington was nicknamed 'Mull-Sack' after the sherry he habitually drank. Having escaped from his apprenticeship as a chimney sweep, aged eight, he became a pickpocket and highwayman with Royalist sympathies. He is alleged to have robbed, among others, Lady Fairfax, the wife of General Fairfax, Oliver Cromwell, and the army pay-wagon of £4,000. He was imprisoned at Newgate and hanged at Smithfield Rounds in 1659.

4   Claude Duval (1643–70)
On the restoration of Charles II to the English throne in 1660, French-born Duval accompanied a band of exiles to London, became a highwayman and the 'most wanted' on a list published in the *London Gazette*. He gained a reputation for gallantry, as an expert cardsharp, gambler and lover. He was captured in the Hole-in-the-Wall Tavern in Chandos Street, near the Strand, London, hanged at Tyburn on 21 January 1670 and buried in St Giles in the Fields – not, as was once believed in St Paul's Covent Garden, with the epitaph: 'Here lies Du Vall: Reader, if Male thou art, Look to thy purse; if Female, to thy heart.'

5   Francis Jackson (d. 1674)
Little is known about Francis Jackson beyond what appears in his own confessions. On 16 March 1674, Jackson and his gang robbed the Windsor Coach between Cranford and Hounslow and two days later held up two coaches between Hounslow and Staines. A hue and cry ensued and after a series of skirmishes he was captured and tried at the Old Bailey. In his cell he dictated his *Recantation* to the Rev. Samuel Smith, the Ordinary of Newgate, before being hanged on 15 April. Jackson's body was hung in chains on a gibbet at North End, Hampstead, to deter others.

6   William Nevison (*c.*1639–84)

Nicknamed 'the Claude Duval of the North', William Nevison – also called John and by various other aliases – was a Yorkshire Royalist highwayman. His most notable exploit was recounted in Daniel Defoe's *A Tour thro' the Whole Island of Great Britain* (1726), where it is claimed that in about 1676 he committed a robbery in Kent and then rode to York at high speed to establish an alibi – an event latter attributed to Dick Turpin. After another incident in 1676, Nevison was sentenced to deportation to Tangier, escaped and was imprisoned in Leicester gaol, but again escaped. In 1684 he was captured near Wakefield and hanged in York on 15 March.

7   William Davis (1627–90)

Known as the 'Golden Farmer' from his habit of paying for everything with gold, Davis, from Wrexham, Denbighshire, moved to Surrey, married well and appeared to be a prosperous farmer, but with 18 children to support, turned to highway robbery, holding up several celebrated figures of the day, including the Duchess of Albemarle. He was finally captured, tried at the Old Bailey and hanged on 22 December 1690, aged 64, and his body was afterwards hung in chains on Bagshot Heath.

8   Dick Turpin (1705–39)

Accounts of Britain's most famous highwaymen vary from those describing him as a gallant rogue to those that consider him a ruthless thug. He was born at Hempstead in Essex, the son of John Turpin, a butcher. After being pursued for cattle rustling, he joined various gangs of smugglers, deer poachers and housebreakers before committing his first highway robbery in July 1735. After a life of crime, he was captured and hanged in York on 7 April 1739. William Harrison Ainsworth's popular novel *Rookwood* (1834) established Turpin as a kind of folk hero and included the (totally untrue) ride to York and references to Turpin's equally apocryphal horse Black Bess.

9   James Maclaine (1724–50)

Known as 'The Gentleman Highwayman', James Maclaine was born in Ireland, the son of a Presbyterian minister. After a number of failed enterprises, he took to the road, wearing a Venetian mask that came to be his trademark. In November 1749, Maclaine robbed the author and politician Horace Walpole and the following year held up the Salisbury Flying Coach near Turnham Green and Lord Eglinton's coach on Hounslow Heath. When items he stole were identified, he was arrested, sentenced to death and hanged on 3 October 1750. His skeleton is displayed in the last of William Hogarth's series of engravings, *The Four Stages of Cruelty* (1751).

10   Jerry Abershaw (*c.*1773–95)

Born in Kingston, Surrey, Louis Jeremiah Abershaw became a highwayman at the age of 17. In January 1795, as he escaped from them, he shot one of his pursuers, David Price. He was subsequently caught and tried at Croydon Assizes and hanged on Kennington Common on 3 August 1795. As he arrived at the gallows, he kicked off his boots to disprove his mother's prophesy that he would die with his boots on. His body was gibbeted on Putney Common. A pamphlet published soon afterwards, *Hardened Villainy Displayed* outlined his short life.

10
BRITISH ROBBERIES

1   Crown Jewels
On 9 May 1671, by befriending the Master of the Jewel House in the Tower of London, Colonel Thomas Blood gained access and stole a crown, orb and sceptre. He was captured but surprisingly was pardoned by Charles II. Blood was later convicted of defamation of the Duke of Buckingham, but died in 1680 before the fine could be recovered. It is claimed that his body was exhumed to ensure he had not faked his own death to evade paying his debt.

2   Great Gold Robbery
On 15 May 1855, a quantity of gold bars and coins, worth over £9 million today, vanished in transit from London Bridge Station to Paris. Several South Eastern Railway officials were arrested for the crime and either jailed or transported to Australia.

3   Stone of Destiny
The Stone of Destiny, or Stone of Scone, was stolen from the Coronation Chair in Westminster Abbey by four young Scottish Nationalists on Christmas Day 1950. It was recovered the following year. Ian Hamilton, one of those responsible for the theft, later became a lawyer and wrote an account of the exploit, *Stone of Destiny*, made into a film released in 2008.

4   Goya portrait of the Duke of Wellington
The portrait was stolen from the National Gallery, London, on 21 August 1961 by Kempton Bunton, an unemployed bus driver. The painting was recovered in a left-luggage office, but Bunton was jailed for stealing the frame. The painting appears on an easel in the lair of Dr No in the 1962 *James Bond* film.

5   Great Train Robbery
Armed robbers stole £2,631,784 from the Glasgow to London Royal Mail train on 8 August 1963. The gang's base, Leatherslade Farm, Buckinghamshire – where they famously played Monopoly with real money – was raided and fingerprints identified, prompting an international manhunt that led to the arrest of 13 gang members, including Ronnie Biggs, who later escaped and lived in Brazil for many years. Ronald 'Buster' Edwards fled to Mexico, but returned to Britain and was jailed; he committed suicide in 1994.

6   Brinks Mat
Posing as security guards, six armed raiders entered the Brinks Mat high-security vault at Heathrow Airport on 26 November 1983 and got away with gold bullion valued at £26 million. Although arrests and convictions followed, most of the haul remains unrecovered.

7   City of London

On 2 May 1990, John Goddard, a messenger in the City of London, was robbed at knife-point of 301 bonds valued at £292 million. Arrests followed and all but two of the bonds were recovered.

8   Leonardo da Vinci's *Madonna with the Yarnwinder*

The painting, valued at over £30 million, was stolen from the Duke of Buccleuch's home, Drumlanrig Castle, Scotland, on 27 August 2003. A £100,000 reward was offered and the work was recovered in 2007.

9   Northern Bank

On 20 December 2004, a gang stole £26.4 million, including banknotes destined for filling ATMs in the days before Christmas, from the HQ of the Northern Bank in Belfast, at the time the largest cash robbery in the UK. The robbers posed as police officers and held family members hostage to force bank officials to admit them to their premises.

10   Securitas depot

On 22 February 2006 raiders carried out the largest ever cash robbery when they stole £53,116,760 from the Securitas depot in Tonbridge, Kent. One man received 20 years and four are serving life sentences for the raid.

BRITISH FAKES AND FORGERIES

1 **George Psalmanazar**
Psalmanazar (1679–1763) fabricated *An Historical and Geographical Description of Formosa* (Taiwan) – a country he had never visited.

2 **Thomas Chatterton**
Bristol-born Chatterton (1752–70) skilfully forged a series of medieval poems as the work of Thomas Rowley. He committed suicide by taking arsenic at the age of 17.

3 **James Macpherson's *Ossian* poems**
In 1760 James Macpherson (1736–96) published a collection of ancient Scottish poems he claimed had been written by Ossian, which have since been shown to be forgeries.

4 **John Payne Collier**
Shakespeare scholar Collier (1789–1883) made changes to Shakespeare texts and forged signatures, as well as works by other writers that he passed off as authentic.

5 **William Henry Ireland**
Ireland (1775–1835) claimed to have discovered a cache of Shakespeare documents, including a 'lost' play, *Vortigern and Rowena*, which was revealed to be a forgery.

6 **Benjamin, Sarpy and Jeffryes**
In 1892, London stamp dealers Alfred Benjamin, Julian Hippolite Sarpy and George Kirke Jeffryes were charged with forging rare stamps and jailed.

7 **Piltdown Man**
Parts of a skull and jawbone allegedly discovered at Piltdown, East Sussex, in 1912 were claimed as the 'missing link' in human evolution, but in 1953 were shown to be fakes. Several people have been identified as the forger, the most likely being Charles Dawson.

8 **Tom Keating**
Keating (1917–84) was one of Britain's most prolific art forgers. Able to work in a wide range of styles, from Rembrandt to Renoir, he was arrested but not tried.

9 ***The Diary of Jack the Ripper***
The diary of James Maybrick (1838–89), published in 1993, pointed to his being Jack the Ripper, but the weight of opinion points to its being a forgery.

10 **Shaun Greenhalgh**
Greenhalgh (b. 1961) forged a diverse range of art, including the Amarna Princess, a statue sold to Bolton Museum for £440,000. In 2007 he was tried and jailed for four years.

UNSOLVED BRITISH MURDERS

1 **Charles Bravo (1876)**
London barrister Bravo was poisoned with antimony. An inquest found he had been murdered and suspicion fell on his wife, Florence, but she was never charged.

2 **'Jack the Ripper' (1888)**
In the space of 70 days, five women were horribly murdered in Whitechapel, London. More than 25 suspects have been named, but the real identity of 'Jack' has never been established.

3 **Caroline Luard (1908)**
Caroline Mary Luard was shot in a summerhouse near Ightham, Kent. Her husband, Major General Luard, committed suicide but her killer was never found.

4 **Bella Wright (1919)**
Known as the 'Green Bicycle Case', Bella Wright of Little Stretton, Leicestershire, was shot. Ronald Light, identified as a man on a bicycle near the crime scene, was tried but acquitted.

5 **Julia Wallace (1931)**
Despite a convincing alibi, William Wallace of Liverpool was found guilty of murdering his wife, Julia, and sentenced to death, but the conviction was overturned.

6 **Brighton trunk murder (1934)**
Part of the body of a woman was discovered in a trunk in the left-luggage office of Brighton Station, and her legs in one at King's Cross. Coincidentally, a second body was found in a trunk in Brighton that year. Tony Mancini was tried but found not guilty of the crime.

7 **'Bible John' (1960s)**
An unknown serial killer who operated in Glasgow in the late 1960s, killing three women, gained his nickname from his supposed religious fervour.

8 **'Jack the Stripper' (1964–5)**
Between six and eight murders in Hammersmith, London, have been attributed to a serial killer who has never been identified.

9 **Suzy Lamplugh (1986)**
Estate agent Lamplugh went missing after apparently showing a client, 'Mr Kipper', a house. No trace of her was ever found and no one has ever been charged with her murder.

10 **Jill Dando (1999)**
TV presenter Dando was shot dead outside her house. Barry George was tried and imprisoned, but successfully appealed and was acquitted in 2008, leaving the case unsolved.

BRITISH EXECUTION LASTS

1 ## Witch executed (1727)
The last people hanged for witchcraft in England were Mary Hicks and her nine-year-old daughter Elizabeth, at Huntingdon on 28 July 1716. The last in Scotland was Janet Horne, burned at the stake at Dornoch on an unknown date in early 1727.

2 ## Beheaded (1747)
Simon Fraser, Lord Lovat, aged 80, was beheaded for treason at Tower Hill, London, on 9 April 1747. As late as 7 November 1817, revolutionaries Jeremiah Brandreth, William Turner and Isaac Ludlum were publicly beheaded *after* being hanged at Nuns Green, Derby, as were the five plotters known as the Cato Street Conspirators (Arthur Thistlewood and his associates), who were publicly hanged and then decapitated with a knife outside Newgate Prison, London, on 1 May 1820.

3 ## Hanged, drawn and quartered (1782)
Found guilty at a Winchester court of spying for the French, David Tyrie was hanged, drawn (disembowelled) and quartered (beheaded and cut into four parts) at Portsmouth on 24 August 1782. James O'Coigley, a Roman Catholic priest, was sentenced to be hanged, drawn and quartered for treason, but was hanged and decapitated only at Pennington Heath, Maidstone, Kent, on 7 June 1798.

4 ## Hanged at Tyburn (1783)
On 7 November 1783, John Austin was the last to be hanged at Tyburn, London, for highway robbery and the murder of John Spicer. The site of Tyburn, near present-day Marble Arch, was used for public hangings from 1196. The three-legged gallows, on which up to 24 criminals could be hanged at once, was set up in 1571. Today, the location is marked by a plaque on a traffic island reading 'The Site of Tyburn Tree'.

5 ## Burned at the stake (1789)
Christian (or Catherine) Murphy (or Bowman), a member of a gang of coiners (forgers) was hanged and then burned at Newgate, London, on 18 March 1789. Coining was considered treason, hence the severity of the sentence – men were customarily hanged, drawn and quartered and women hanged and burned. This form of capital punishment was abolished on 5 June 1790.

6   Hanged at Execution Dock (1830)

The low water of Execution Dock, Wapping, London, was the site of the gallows used to hang pirates, including the notorious Captain Kidd in 1701. After being hanged, the tide was allowed to immerse the bodies three times before they were cut down. The last to receive this punishment were William Watts and George Davis on 16 December 1830.

7   Public hanging (1868)

Michael Barrett was publicly hanged outside Newgate Prison, London, on 26 May 1868 for the murder of Sarah Ann Hodgkinson during a Fenian (Irish nationalist) bombing in Clerkenwell the previous year in which 12 people were killed and 120 seriously injured. Barrett's body was buried within the prison, but in 1903 his remains were reburied in the City of London Cemetery.

8   Executed at the Tower of London (1941)

Josef Jakobs (b. 30 June 1898), a German spy, parachuted into Huntingdonshire with a radio transmitter, but injured his leg in the descent and was captured by the Home Guard. He was tried and shot at the Tower of London on 15 August 1941, seated in a chair. His body was buried in an unmarked grave in St Mary's Roman Catholic Cemetery, Kensal Green, London.

9   Woman hanged (1955)

Ruth Ellis, the last woman to be hanged in the UK, was executed at Holloway Prison, London, on 13 July 1955 for shooting David Blakely. Originally buried inside the prison, her remains were later reburied at St Mary's Church, Amersham, Buckinghamshire.

10   Men hanged (1964)

Peter Anthony Allen was hanged at Liverpool and John Robson Welby (aka Gwynne Owen Evans) at Manchester at 8 a.m. on 13 August 1964. Both men had been found guilty of stabbing John Alan West to death during a robbery. Capital punishment was abolished in the UK on 9 November 1965.

THE 10
WORST CONFLICTS
for UK military casualties*

	Campaign	Military dead†
1	First World War (1914–18)	956,703
2	Second World War (1939–45)	382,600
3	Crimean War (1854–6)	22,182
4	Second Boer War (1899–1902)	22,000
5	First Anglo-Afghan War (1839–42)	5,062
6	Anglo-Zulu War (1879)	1,673
7	Third Anglo-Afghan War (1919)	1,136
8	Korean War (1950–53)	1,109
9	Russian Civil War (1918–20)	1,073
10	Second Anglo-Afghan War (1878–80)	1,057

* 1815–present
† Total under British command killed in action, died of wounds, disease or injury and missing presumed dead

WORST BATTLES
on British soil

Battle/combatants/date	Estimated casualties
1 **Location unknown, Iceni vs. Romans,** AD 61 Some 80,000 Britons under Queen Boadicea of the Iceni were alleged to have been killed, with the loss of just 400 Romans.	80,400
2 **Towton, Yorkists vs. Lancastrians, 29 Mar 1461** At least 28,000 were reckoned to have been killed in what was reputedly the bloodiest battle on English soil since Roman times.	>28,000
3 **Flodden, Scots vs. English, 9 Sep 1513** 10,000 Scots were killed, with similarly heavy losses on the English side.	20,000
4 **Bannockburn, Scots vs. English, 24 Jun 1314** English losses were put at some 15,000, those of the Scots about 4,000.	19,000
5 **Lewes, Simon de Montfort vs. Henry III, 14 May 1264** The precise figure is unknown, but estimates range from 10,000 to 40,000.	10–40,000
6 **Dunbar, English vs. Scots, 27 Apr 1296** The Scottish were defeated with a (probably exaggerated) loss of 10,000 troops.	>10,000
7 **Neville's Cross (Durham), English vs. Scots, 17 Oct 1346** The Scots were defeated with losses of about 75 per cent – almost 9,000 soldiers.	9,000
8 **Naseby, Royalists vs. Parliamentarians, 14 Jun 1645** A high proportion of the Royalist army of 9,000 was wiped out.	7,500
9 **Evesham, Crown vs. Barons, 4 Aug 1265** Simon de Montfort's baronial army of 5,350 was annihilated.	7,000
10 **Falkirk, English vs. Scots, 22 Jul 1298** About 5,000 Scots and 200 English were said to have been killed, the disparity resulting from the superiority of the English archers.	>5,000

Perhaps the most famous of all British battles, Hastings (Saxons vs. Normans, 14 October 1066), does not qualify for this list. Both sides had approximately 7,000 troops and losses were said to have been about a quarter on each side, hence a total killed of around 3,500 has been suggested. This list is inevitably non-definitive, since no precise figures for losses are available, particularly for early battles, and some are exaggerated for political advantage.

THE 10
LAST BATTLES
on British soil

Battle	Date
1 **Culloden** Royalist troops under the Duke of Cumberland defeated a force of Jacobites.	16 Apr 1746
2 **Falkirk** The last Jacobite victory against the British army.	17 Jan 1746
3 **Prestonpans** Jacobite victory over Royal troops.	21 Sep 1745
4 **Inverurie** A Hanoverian force under MacLeod of MacLeod was defeated by a superior Jacobite army under Lord Lewis Gordon.	23 Dec 1745
5 **Glen Shiel** The British defeated a Jacobite and Spanish army.	10 Jun 1719
6 **Sheriffmuir** Royal troops under the Duke of Argyll were routed by a superior force of Highlanders under the Earl of Mar.	13 Nov 1715
7 **Boyne** The army of the deposed king, James II, was defeated by that of William III.	1 Jul 1690*
8 **Killiecrankie** The Royalist army under General Mackay was defeated by a smaller force of Highland Jacobites.	27 Jul 1689
9 **Dunkeld** Highlanders under Colonel Cannon retreated after he was killed in a battle with the Cameronian Regiment under the Marquis of Atholl.	21 Aug 1689
10 **Reading** The last battle – more a skirmish – on English soil, when James II attempted to resist the Dutch army of William and Mary.	9 Dec 1688

* **Commemorated as 12 July due to calendar change**
It could be argued that the Battle of Britain (10 July–3 October 1940) took place above British soil.

THE 10
WORST ALLIED BATTLE OF BRITAIN LOSSES

	Service or nationality	Pilots	Killed
1	RAF (British/other Commonwealth)	1,822	339
2	Polish	141	29
3	Canadian	88	20
4	Australian	21	14
5	New Zealander	73	11
6=	Fleet Air Arm	56	9
=	South African	21	9
8	Czech	86	8
9	Belgian	26	6
10	American	7	1

MOST HEAVILY BLITZED CITIES
in the UK

	City	Major raids	Tonnage of high explosive dropped
1	London	85	23,949
2	Liverpool/Birkenhead	8	1,957
3	Birmingham	8	1,852
4	Glasgow/Clydeside	5	1,329
5	Plymouth/Devonport	8	1,228
6	Bristol/Avonmouth	6	919
7	Coventry	2	818
8	Portsmouth	3	687
9	Southampton	4	647
10	Hull	3	593

The list, which is derived from official German sources, is based on total tonnage of high explosive dropped in major night attacks during the Blitz period, from 7 September 1940 until 16 May 1941. Further urban centres – Manchester, Belfast, Sheffield, Newcastle/Tyneside, Nottingham and Cardiff – were also victims of significant air raids in the same period.

BRITISH BUILDINGS DESTROYED IN THE BLITZ

1   ## Coventry Cathedral
Once Britain's largest parish church, it gained cathedral status in 1918, but was destroyed, with the exception of its tower and outer wall, in an air raid on 14 November 1940.

2   ## Great Synagogue of London
The last of several synagogues built on the site in Duke's Place was completed in 1790 and destroyed on 10 May 1941 during London's raid.

3   ## St Dunstan-in-the-East
The church in the City of London was designed by Sir Christopher Wren. On 10 May 1941, all but its steeple was destroyed. The site is now a garden, opened in 1971.

4   ## St Luke's Church, Liverpool
Built in 1831, its interior was destroyed by an incendiary bomb in an air raid on 5 May 1941, only its spire and outer walls surviving.

5   ## St Mary Aldermanbury
The Wren church was gutted by an incendiary bomb on 29 December 1940. Its ruins were dismantled and rebuilt in 1965–69 as a memorial to Winston Churchill at Westminster College, Fulton, Missouri – where Churchill had made his famous 'Iron Curtain' speech.

6   ## Shaftesbury Theatre
The Shaftesbury Theatre in Shaftesbury Avenue, London, opened in 1888. It was destroyed by bombing on 17 April 1941 – a fire station now occupies its site.

7   ## Britannia Theatre, Hoxton, London
Converted from a public house to a theatre in the 1850s and to a cinema in 1913, it suffered bombing in 1940 and its remains were demolished in 1941.

8   ## Pollock's Toy Museum, Hoxton, London
The museum established by Benjamin Pollock (1856–1937), printer of Victorian toy theatres, was destroyed in the same raid as that which destroyed the Britannia Theatre.

9   ## Christ Church Greyfriars, London
The large church in Newgate Street, rebuilt by Wren in 1687, was almost totally destroyed on 29 December 1940.

10 ## London Necropolis railway station
The station, near London's Waterloo Station, opened in 1854 to transport bodies from London to the London Necropolis, Surrey. It was destroyed by bombing on 16 April 1941.

THE 10

CAMPAIGNS IN WHICH MOST VICTORIA CROSSES have been won

	Campaign	VCs
1	First World War (1914–18)	634
2=	Indian Mutiny (1857–8)	182
=	Second World War (1939–45)	182
4	Crimean War (1854–6)	111
5	Second Boer War (1899–1902)	78
6	Zulu War (1879)	23
7	Second Anglo-Afghan War (1878–80)	16
8	Waikato-Hauhau Maori War (1863–6)	13
9=	Third China War (1860)	7
=	Tirah Campaign, India (1897–8)	7

The Royal Warrant inaugurating the Victoria Cross, Britain's highest gallantry award, was signed on 29 January 1856, but actions dating back to 1854 were included, hence encompassing the Crimean campaign. The names of the first recipients were announced in the *London Gazette* on 24 February 1857 and the first investiture of 62 men was held on 26 June 1857 in Hyde Park, London, with Queen Victoria herself presenting the medals. The occasion marked two further 'firsts': it was the first time that both officers and men had received the same award, and the first when both had been present at the same ceremony. The sole criterion for receiving a VC was described as 'the merit of conspicuous bravery', later modified to 'most conspicuous bravery or some daring pre-eminent act of valour or self-sacrifice or extreme devotion to duty in the presence of the enemy'. These 10 campaigns account for all but 102 of the 1,355 VCs ever awarded, up to that of Bryan Budd of the Parachute Regiment's posthumous 2006 award during the Afghanistan campaign, the 14th since the Second World War. The youngest ever recipient of a VC was Andrew Fitzgibbon, for an action at Taku Forts, China, on 21 August 1860, when he was aged 15 years, 3 months and 8 days.

BRITAIN:
A VISITOR'S
GUIDE

BRITISH CITIES MOST VISITED BY OVERSEAS TOURISTS

	City	Total spending	Estimated overseas visitors (2006)
1	London	£7,822,000,000	15,593,000
2	Edinburgh	£484,000,000	1,338,000
3	Manchester	£335,000,000	912,000
4	Birmingham	£243,000,000	779,000
5	Glasgow	£241,000,000	741,000
6	Liverpool	£198,000,000	625,000
7	Oxford	£193,000,000	449,000
8	Bristol	£129,000,000	403,000
9	Cardiff	£127,000,000	355,000
10	Cambridge	£149,000,000	348,000

Source: National Statistics

TOURIST ATTRACTIONS
in the UK

	Attraction/location	Visitors (2007)
1	Blackpool Pleasure Beach, Blackpool	5,500,000
2	British Museum, London	5,418,265
3	Tate Modern, London	5,191,840
4	National Gallery, London	4,159,485
5	Natural History Museum, London	3,600,119
6	London Eye, London	3,500,000
7	Science Museum, London	2,714,021
8	Alton Towers, Staffordshire	2,400,000
9	Victoria and Albert Museum, London	2,435,300
10	Tower of London, London	2,064,126

Source: Association of Leading Visitor Attractions (ALVA)/London Eye

LARGEST AREAS OF OUTSTANDING NATURAL BEAUTY in England and Wales

	Area/established	Size
1	Cotswolds (Aug 1966/Dec 1990)	2,038 sq km (787 sq miles)
2	North Pennines (Jun 1988)	1,983 sq km (766 sq miles)
3	North Wessex Downs (Dec 1972)	1,730 sq km (668 sq miles)
4	High Weald (Oct 1983)	1,460 sq km (564 sq miles)
5	Dorset (Jul 1959)	1,129 sq km (436 sq miles)
6=	Sussex Downs (Apr 1966)	983 sq km (380 sq miles)
=	Cranborne Chase and West Wiltshire Downs (Oct 1983)	983 sq km (380 sq miles)
8	Cornwall (Nov 1959/Oct 1983)	958 sq km (370 sq miles)
9	Kent Downs (Jul 1968)	878 sq km (339 sq miles)
10	Chilterns (Dec 1965/Mar 1990)	833 sq km (322 sq miles)

Source: National Association for AONBs

England and Wales have 40 Areas of Outstanding Natural Beauty (35 wholly in England, four in Wales and one straddling the border), comprising a total of 21,237 sq km (8,200 sq miles), with 20,393 sq km (7,874 sq miles) in England and 844 sq km (326 sq miles) in Wales. This represents some 14 per cent of the total area of the two countries. There are also nine Areas of Outstanding Natural Beauty in Northern Ireland and 40 National Scenic Areas designated in Scotland, occupying some 10,018 sq km (3,867 sq miles). The Isles of Scilly AONB, designated in 1975, is the smallest at 16 sq km (6 sq miles).

FIRST UNESCO WORLD
HERITAGE SITES in the UK

Site	Year
1= The Giant's Causeway and Causeway Coast	1986
= Durham Castle and Cathedral	1986
= Ironbridge Gorge	1986
= Studley Royal Park, including the Ruins of Fountains Abbey	1986
= Stonehenge, Avebury and associated sites	1986
= The Castles and Town Walls of King Edward in Gwynedd	1986
= St Kilda	1986
8= Blenheim Palace	1987
= City of Bath	1987
= Hadrian's Wall	1987
= Palace of Westminster, Abbey of Westminster and St Margaret's Church	1987

UNESCO (United Nations Educational, Scientific and Cultural Organization) has been identifying World Heritage sites since 1978. Sites are structures or locations – cultural, natural or mixed – considered, according to a set of criteria, worthy of conserving for humanity. A total of 24 have been listed in the UK, with others in overseas dependencies, the most recent being Liverpool's dockland area (2004) and Cornwall and West Devon mining landscape (2006).

ART GALLERIES AND MUSEUMS
in the UK

	Attraction/location	Visitors (2007)
1	British Museum, London	5,418,265
2	Tate Modern, London	5,191,840
3	National Gallery, London	4,159,485
4	Natural History Museum, London	3,600,119
5	Science Museum, London	2,714,021
6	Victoria and Albert Museum, London	2,435,300
7	National Maritime Museum, London	1,695,739
8	National Portrait Gallery, London	1,607,767
9	Tate Britain, London	1,593,277
10	British Library, London	1,355,425

TOP 10

LARGEST NATIONAL PARKS
in the UK

	National Park/established	Area
1	Cairngorms (1 Sep 2003)	3,800 sq km (1,467 sq miles)
2	Lake District (9 May 1951)	2,292 sq km (885 sq miles)
3	Snowdonia (18 Oct 1951)	2,142 sq km (827 sq miles)
4	Loch Lomond and the Trossachs (19 Jul 2002)	1,865 sq km (720 sq miles)
5	Yorkshire Dales (13 Oct 1954)	1,769 sq km (683 sq miles)
6	Peak District (17 Apr 1951)	1,438 sq km (555 sq miles)
7	North York Moors (28 Nov 1952)	1,436 sq km (554 sq miles)
8	Brecon Beacons (17 Apr 1957)	1,351 sq km (522 sq miles)
9	Northumberland (6 Apr 1956)	1,049 sq km (405 sq miles)
10	Dartmoor (30 Oct 1951/14 Apr 1994)	954 sq km (368 sq miles)

Source: Association of National Park Authorities (ANPA)

Following the National Parks and Access to the Countryside Act of 1949, Britain's first National Parks were established in the 1950s to conserve and protect some of the most picturesque landscapes of England and Wales from unsuitable development, at the same time allowing the public free access to them. Exmoor, the Pembrokeshire coast, the Broads (the smallest at 303 sq km/117 sq miles) and the New Forest (the latest, designated 1 March 2005: 580 sq km/224 sq miles) complete the list. The South Downs (1,641 sq km/634 sq miles) is scheduled to become a National Park in 2009.

LARGEST HILL FIGURES
in the UK*

	Figure/location	Length†
1	Whipsnade White Lion, Bedfordshire	147 m (483 ft)
2	Uffington White Horse, Oxfordshire	114 m (374 ft)
3	Osmington White Horse, Dorset	98 m (323 ft)
4	Kilburn White Horse, Yorkshire	97 m (318 ft)
5	Folkestone White Horse, Kent	81 m (267 ft)
6	Long Man of Wilmington, East Sussex	69 m (227 ft)
7	Cherhill White Horse, Wiltshire	67 m (220 ft)
8	Westbury White Horse, Wiltshire	55.5 m (182 ft)
9	Cerne Abbas Giant, Dorset	54.9 m (180 ft)
10	Alton Barnes White Horse, Wiltshire	51 m (166 ft)

* Figures only, excluding military badges, crosses, etc
† Longest dimension

The carving of giant horses (sometimes called leucipotomy), and figures (gigantotomy) in the British landscape, especially in chalk and limestone areas where the image contrasts with the darker surrounding soil or grass, has been carried out since ancient times – the Uffington White Horse is claimed to date back some 3,000 years. A variety of geoglyph or earth carving, there are some 57 such images in Britain, although without periodic maintenance and scouring, many others have vanished.

LARGEST ROYAL PARKS
in the UK

	Park	Area
1	Richmond Park, Surrey	955 hectares (2,360 acres)
2	Hampton Court Park and Gardens, Surrey	669 hectares (1,653 acres)
3	Bushey Park, Middlesex	445 hectares (1,099 acres)
4	Regent's Park, London	166 hectares (410 acres)
5	Hyde Park, London	142 hectares (350 acres)
6	Royal Botanic Gardens, Kew, Surrey	120 hectares (300 acres)
7	Kensington Gardens, London	111 hectares (275 acres)
8	Greenwich Park, London	74 hectares (183 acres)
9	St James's Park, London	23 hectares (58 acres)
10	Green Park, London	19 hectares (47 acres)

TOP 10

MOST-VISITED NATIONAL TRUST PROPERTIES in the UK

	Property	Visitors (2007–8)
1	Wakehurst Place, West Sussex	477,173
2	Waddesdon Manor, Buckinghamshire	386,544
3	Stourhead House and Garden, Wiltshire	382,271
4	Fountains Abbey and Studley Royal, North Yorkshire	348,725
5	Polesden Lacey, Surrey	258,310
6	Larrybane/Carrick-a-Rede rope bridge, Antrim, Northern Ireland	222,613
7	Penrhyn Castle, Gwynedd	212,727
8	Belton House, Lincolnshire	212,256
9	St Michael's Mount, Cornwall	203,798
10	Sheffield Park Garden, East Sussex	202,940

MOST-VISITED HISTORIC
PROPERTIES in the UK

	Property	Visits (2007)
1	Tower of London, London	2,064,126
2	St Paul's Cathedral, London	1,623,881
3	Edinburgh Castle, Edinburgh	1,229,703
4	Windsor Castle and Frogmore House, Berkshire	1,003,000
5	Houses of Parliament, London	994,926
6	Roman Baths and Pump Room, Bath, Somerset	985,096
7	Stonehenge, Wiltshire	869,432
8	Warwick Castle, Warwick	750,000
9	Shakespeare's Birthplace, Stratford-upon-Avon, Warwickshire	688,000
10	Chatsworth House, Derbyshire	606,500

BRITISH CEMETERIES
and their famous inhabitants

1   Brookwood, Woking, Surrey
Founded in 1852, Brookwood, or the London Necropolis, had its own railway connection
to London. Once the world's largest cemetery, it contains some 240,000 graves, among
them those of Saxon king Edward the Martyr (d. 978), American-born painter John Singer
Sargent (d. 1925) and novelist Dame Rebecca West (d. 1983). It also contains a First World
War American cemetery, Britain's oldest Muslim cemetery and a Zoroastrian burial
ground.

2   Bunhill Fields, London
A burial ground for London's Nonconformists from 1665 onwards, it is the last resting
place of *Pilgrim's Progress* author John Bunyan (d. 1688), Quakers founder George Fox
(d. 1691), *Robinson Crusoe* author Daniel Defoe (d. 1731), the composer of the hymn
'O God Our Help in Ages Past' Isaac Watts (d. 1748) and poet and painter William Blake
(d. 1827).

3   Royal Burial Ground, Frogmore, Berkshire
Queen Victoria and Prince Albert are buried in the Mausoleum, but other royals lie in the
Burial Ground, including three of Victoria's children, as well as the Duke and Duchess of
Windsor (Edward VIII and Wallis Simpson).

4   Highgate, London
The cemetery contains the much-visited tomb of Karl Marx (d. 1883), painter Dante
Gabriel Rossetti's wife Elizabeth Siddal (d. 1862) – whose grave he famously had opened in
1869 to retrieve a book of poems he had placed in her coffin, pioneer film-maker William
Friese-Greene (d. 1921), dog-show founder Charles Cruft (d. 1938), actor Sir Ralph
Richardson (d. 1983) and comedian Max Wall (d. 1990). Among recent internments are
those of *The Hitchiker's Guide to the Galaxy* author Douglas Adams (d. 2001), journalist
Paul Foot (d. 2004) and actress Sheila Gish (d. 2005).

5   Kensal Green, London
The diverse inhabitants of this large London cemetery include engineer Isambard
Kingdom Brunel (d. 1859), newsagent W. H. Smith (d. 1865), computer pioneer Charles
Babbage (d. 1871), tightrope walker Charles Blondin (d. 1897), novelists William
Thackeray (d. 1863), Anthony Trollope (d. 1882) and Wilkie Collins (d. 1889), and
Major Walter Wingfield (d. 1912), the inventor of lawn tennis. One of its most curious
incumbents is James Barry, who served in the British army as a surgeon, but on whose
death in 1865 was discovered to be a woman. Modern graves include those of fashion
designer Ossie Clarke (d. 1996) and the journalist husband of Nigella Lawson, John
Diamond (d. 2001).

6 Iona Abbey, Scotland

Duncan, the Scottish king murdered by Macbeth in 1140, is reputed to be buried here, along with 47 other Scottish kings, a number of Scottish saints and John Smith, the Labour Party leader, who died in 1994.

7 St Martin, Bladon, Oxfordshire

The simple tomb of Sir Winston Churchill, buried here in 1965 after the last non-royal state funeral in Britain, shares the cemetery with his wife, Clementine, his mother and other Churchill family members.

8 Golders Green Crematorium, London

While many notable people have been cremated here and their ashes scattered elsewhere, the ashes of some were either buried in the grounds or remain in urns in the Columbarium. Among them are those of *Dracula* author Bram Stoker (d. 1912), writer Rudyard Kipling (d. 1936), psychiatrist Sigmund Freud (d. 1939), *Carry On* star Sid James (d. 1976), T. Rex singer Marc Bolan (d. 1977), Who drummer Keith Moon (d. 1978), actor Peter Sellers (d. 1980) and publisher Paul Hamlyn (d. 2001).

9 West Norwood, Surrey

This large cemetery was established in 1837 to cope with the burials from an expanding London. It contains over 164,000 graves, including those of cookery writer Mrs (Isabella) Beeton, who died in 1865, aged 28, Tower Bridge architect Sir Horace Jones (d. 1887), Tate Gallery founder Sir Henry Tate (d. 1899) and machine-gun inventor Sir Hiram Maxim (d. 1916).

10 St Peter, Bournemouth, Dorset

Women's rights pioneer Mary Wollstonecraft (d. 1797)and her husband, William Godwin (d. 1836), were buried here, along with their daughter, Mary Shelley (d. 1851), the author of *Frankenstein* – together with the heart of her husband, the poet Percy Shelley (d. 1822). Other graves include that of the inventor of the Bailey bridge, Sir Ronald Bailey (d. 1985).

10
BRITISH MAZES

Maze/location (type)

1 Breamore, Hampshire (turf)
One of eight surviving turf mizmazes in Britain, the 13th-century Breamore maze measures 26 × 25 m (84 × 81 ft).

2 Hampton Court Palace (hedge)
Planted for William of Orange in about 1690, the 68 × 25 m (222 × 82 ft) maze features in Jerome K. Jerome's *Three Men in a Boat* (1889) – in which the trio get lost.

3 Glendurgan Maze, near Falmouth, Cornwall (hedge)
The maze dates from 1833 and covers 41 × 22 m (133 × 108 ft).

4 Hazlehead Maze, Aberdeen (hedge)
The maze, in Hazlehead Park, was built by Sir Henry Alexander in 1935 and measures 58 × 49 m (190 × 160 ft).

5 Longleat, Wiltshire (hedge)
Designed by Greg Bright in 1978, it is 116 × 53 m (380 × 175 ft) with 2.7 km (1.69 miles) of paths.

6 Blenheim Palace Hedge Maze, Oxfordshire (hedge)
Designed by Adrian Fisher and Randoll Coate in 1991, the yew maze measures 90 × 56 m (294 × 185 ft).

7 Greys Court 'Archbishop's Maze', Oxfordshire (brick and grass)
Designed by Adrian Fisher and opened by the Archbishop of Canterbury in 1981, it measures 26 × 26 m (85 × 85 ft).

8 Leeds Castle, Maidstone, Kent (hedge)
Designed by Adrian Fisher, Randoll Coate and Vernon Gibberd in 1988, the 48 × 48 m (156 × 156 ft) maze has a stone tower and an underground grotto.

9 Peace Maze, Castlewellan Forest Park, Northern Ireland (hedge)
Opened in 2001, it is one of the largest mazes in the UK, with 6,000 yew trees covering an area of 11,000 sq m (118,403 sq ft).

10 Noah's Ark Zoo Farm, Bristol (hedge)
Planted with 14,000 beech trees in 2003, its 3.2 km (2 miles) of paths make it one of the longest hedge mazes in the world.

TALLEST HABITABLE* BUILDINGS
in the UK

	Building/location/year completed	Storeys	Roof height
1	One Canada Square, Canary Wharf, London, 1991	50	235.1 m (771 ft)
2=	8 Canada Square (HSBC Tower), Canary Wharf, London, 2002	45	199.5 m (655 ft)
=	25 Canada Square (Citigroup Centre), Canary Wharf, London, 2001	45	199.5 m (655 ft)
4	Tower 42 (formerly National Westminster Tower), London, 1980	47	183 m (600 ft)
5	30 St Mary Axe ('The Gherkin'), London, 2004	41	179.8 m (590 ft)
6	Broadgate Tower, London, 2008	36	164.3 m (539 ft)
7	Beetham Tower, Manchester, 2006	50	157 m (515 ft)
8	1 Churchill Place, London, 2004	32	156.4 m (513 ft)
9=	25 Bank Street, London, 2003	33	153 m (502 ft)
=	40 Bank Street, London, 2003	33	153 m (502 ft)

* Excluding communications masts, towers, chimneys and church spires

TALLEST CATHEDRALS AND CHURCHES in the UK

	Church/location/type/year completed	Height
1	Salisbury Cathedral, Wiltshire (spire), 1310	123 m (404 ft)
2	St Paul's Cathedral, London (dome), 1710	112 m (366 ft)
3	Liverpool Anglican Cathedral, Merseyside (tower), 1942	101 m (331 ft)
4	Norwich Cathedral, Norfolk (spire), 1465	96 m (315 ft)
5	St Walburge Catholic Church, Preston, Lancashire (spire), 1854	94 m (309 ft)
6	Canterbury Cathedral, Kent (tower), 1510	91 m (297 ft)
7=	Coventry (Old) Cathedral, West Midlands (spire*), 1433	90 m (295 ft)
=	St James's Church, Louth, Lincolnshire (spire), 1515	90 m (295 ft)
=	St Mary's Episcopal Cathedral, Edinburgh Scotland (spire), 1917	90 m (295 ft)
10	St Mary Redcliffe, Bristol, Avon (spire), 1872	89 m (292 ft)

* The spire survived the bombing of 14 November 1940 that destroyed the cathedral

BRITISH TOWERS

1   Grimsby Dock Tower, Lincolnshire
    Designed by James William Wild and built in 1852 as a water tower to provide hydraulic
    power for the docks, the 94-m (309-ft) tower was once Britain's tallest secular building.

2   Great Tower of London, Wembley
    Partly constructed in 1891 and intended to be 350.5 m (1,150 ft) – 50 m (165 ft) taller than
    the Eiffel Tower, it was abandoned in 1894 and Wembley Stadium built on the site.

3   Blackpool Tower, Lancashire
    Modelled on the Eiffel Tower and opened in 1894, the much-visited 158-m (518-ft 9-in)
    steel tower features a range of entertainment facilities.

4   New Brighton Tower, Merseyside
    The 172.8-m (567-ft) tower was built in 1896–1900, but dismantled in 1919–21. The
    ballroom at its base was a concert venue where acts such as the Beatles performed, but was
    destroyed by fire in 1969.

5   BT Tower, London
    Formerly the Post Office Tower, the 177-m (581-ft) structure, originally with a rotating
    restaurant, was opened in 1966.

6   British Telecom Tower, Birmingham
    Opened in 1967, the 152-m (500-ft) tower, topped by an array of antennae, is currently the
    tallest structure in the city of Birmingham.

7   Radio City Tower (St John's Beacon), Liverpool
    Built, but never used, as a ventilation shaft, the 102-m (335-ft) tower was completed in
    1968 and featured a revolving restaurant. It is now occupied by radio stations.

8   Emley Moor Transmitter
    Completed in 1971, the 594-m (1,949-ft) transmitter, with an observatory at 275 m
    (902 ft), is Britain's tallest free-standing tower.

9   Science Centre Tower, Glasgow
    Scotland's tallest tower, and the tallest in the world where the whole tower rotates
    360 degrees, the 127-m (417-ft) structure was completed in 2001.

10 Spinnaker Tower, Portsmouth
    The sail-shaped 170-m (558-ft) tower was completed in 2005 and in its first year attracted
    over 600,000 visitors.

FASTEST ROLLER COASTERS
in the UK

	Roller coaster	Speed
1	**Stealth** Thorpe Park, Surrey 2006	129 km/h (80.0 mph)
2	**Pepsi Max Big One** Blackpool Pleasure Beach 1994	119 km/h (74.0 mph)
3	**Oblivion** Alton Towers, Staffordshire 1998	109 km/h (68.0 mph)
4	**Jubilee Odyssey** Fantasy Island, Lincolnshire 2002	101 km/h (63.0 mph)
5	**Rita – Queen of Speed** Alton Towers, Staffordshire 2005	98 km/h (61.1 mph)
6	**Speed: No Limits** Oakwood Theme Park, Pembrokeshire 2006	97 km/h (60.0 mph)
7	**Millennium Roller Coaster** Fantasy Island, Lincolnshire 1999	90 km/h (55.9 mph)
8	**Kumali** Flamingo Land Theme Park & Zoo, Yorkshire 2006	88 km/h (54.9 mph)
9	**Velocity** Flamingo Land Theme Park & Zoo, Yorkshire 2005	87 km/h (54.0 mph)
10	**Shockwave** Drayton Manor Park, Staffordshire 1995	85 km/h (53.0 mph)

LONGEST SEASIDE PIERS
in the UK

	Pier	Built*	Length
1	Southend-on-Sea, Essex	1890	2,158 m (7,080 ft)
2	Southport, Lancashire†	1860	1,107.3 m (3,633 ft)
3	Walton-on-the-Naze, Essex	1895	792.5 m (2,600 ft)
4	Ryde, Isle of Wight	1814	702.6 m (2,305 ft)
5	Llandudno, Gwynedd	1878	699.5 m (2,295 ft)
6	Ramsey, Isle of Man	1882	683.1 m (2,241 ft)
7	Hythe, Hampshire	1881	640.1 m (2,100 ft)
8	Brighton (Palace Pier), East Sussex	1901	536.5 m (1,760 ft)
9	Bangor (Garth Pier), Gwynedd	1896	472.4 m (1,550 ft)
10	Weston-super-Mare (Birnbeck Pier), Avon‡	1867	411.5 m (1,350 ft)

* Some have since been extended
† Formerly the longest at 1,335 m (4,380 ft) in 1868
‡ Burned 28 July 2008, but standing
Source: National Piers Society

STEAM RAILWAYS
in the UK

1 **Bluebell Railway**
Part of the former Lewes and East Grinstead Railway, the 14.5-km (9-mile) Bluebell line is the world's first preserved standard-gauge steam railway, opened on 7 August 1960.

2 **Ffestiniog Railway**
Built to serve the local slate industry, the narrow-gauge railway operates 21.7 km (13.5 miles) of track in Snowdonia, from Porthmadog to Blaenau Ffestiniog.

3 **Isle of Man Steam Railway**
The last 24.6-km (15.3-mile) section of the Isle of Man's once extensive narrow-gauge railway runs between Douglas and Port Erin.

4 **Isle of Wight Steam Railway**
The 8.9-km (5.5-mile) standard-gauge railway has been run by volunteers since 1971, using steam engines that formerly ran on the Isle's network.

5 **Middleton Railway**
Although operating only a short service over 1.6 km (1 mile) of track, it is the world's oldest-established railway company, having run horse-drawn trucks as early as 1758.

6 **Romney, Hythe & Dymchurch Railway**
Inaugurated on 16 July 1927, this narrow-gauge railway runs for 21.7 km (13.5 miles) between Hythe and Dungeness, Kent.

7 **Strathspey Railway**
Running between Aviemore and Broomhill in the Scottish Highlands, a distance of 16 km (10 miles), it operates both steam and diesel engines.

8 **Talyllyn Railway**
Operating from Tywyn to Nant Gwernol, a distance of 11.7 km (7.3 miles), it became in 1865 the first narrow-gauge railway licensed to carry passengers and in 1951 the first to be preserved and operated by volunteers.

9 **Tanfield Railway**
Running on a 9.7-km (6-mile) line in country Durham, it was originally a colliery line, employing horse-drawn trucks in 1725, making it the world's oldest working railway.

10 **West Somerset Railway**
Operating between Bishops Lydeard and Watchet, it is the longest privately owned standard-gauge heritage railway in Britain, with 37 km (23 miles) of track.

OLDEST MOUNTAIN AND FUNICULAR RAILWAYS in the UK

	Railway	Opened
1	Saltburn Cliff Railway, Redcar and Cleveland	28 Jun 1884
2	Lynton and Lynmouth Cliff Railway, Lynton, Devon	19 Apr 1890
3	West Hill Cliff Railway, Hastings, East Sussex	28 Aug 1891
4	Bridgnorth Cliff Railway, Shropshire	7 Jul 1892
5	Shipley Glen Cable Tramway, West Yorkshire	18 May 1895
6	Snaefell Mountain Railway, Isle of Man	20 Aug 1895
7	Snowdon Mountain Railway, Llanberis, Gwynedd	6 Apr 1896
8	Aberystwyth Cliff Railway, Aberystwyth, Ceredigion	1 Aug 1896
9	Great Orme Tramway, Llandudno, Conwy	31 Jul 1902
10	East Hill Cliff Railway, Hastings, East Sussex	10 Aug 1902

UNDERGROUND SITES
in Britain

1 **Gough's Cave, Somerset**

Part of Cheddar Gorge, Gough's Cave was discovered in 1890 by Richard Cox Gough (1827–1902). It is a prehistoric cavern with chambers containing a variety of stalactites, stalagmites and rock formations, extending some 2.1 km (1.3 miles) at a depth of 90 m (295 ft). A carving of a mammoth and the skeleton of Cheddar Man, Britain's earliest-known human remains, dating back some 7,150 years, have been found in the cave.

2 **Chislehurst Caves, Greater London**

Extending some 35 km (22 miles), the manmade caves were constructed as an ancient lime and flint mine. They were used as an arms store in the First World War, as a mushroom farm, an air raid shelter in the Second World War, for rock concerts in the 1960s and in 1973 as the setting for an episode of *Doctor Who*.

3 **West Wycombe Caves, Buckinghamshire**

In the 18th century the caves, also known as the Hell-Fire Caves, were notable as the meeting place and venue for the orgies of the notorious Hellfire Club, presided over by Sir Francis Dashwood (1708–81), owner of nearby West Wycombe Park (now a National Trust property). Created by extending an existing chalk mine, the caves feature a series of 'rooms' including an Entrance Hall, Circle, Franklin's Cave (named after Benjamin Franklin), Banqueting Hall, Triangle and Miner's Cave, a subterranean river, the Styx, and the Inner Temple. They are now open to the public.

4 **Williamson's Tunnels, Liverpool**

In the early 19th century Joseph Williamson (1769–1840), a Liverpool businessman known as The Mole of Edge Hill, paid for a vast network of tunnels to be constructed, probably to provide employment for the poor of the area. They are undergoing restoration and are open to the public.

5 **Welbeck Abbey, Nottinghamshire**

William John Cavendish Cavendish-Scott-Bentinck, 5th Duke of Portland (1800–79), was the eccentric owner of Welbeck Abbey. Living as a recluse in a small suite of rooms in the massive abbey, he employed a team of hundreds of workmen to excavate a series of underground rooms, including a 53-m (174-ft) long ballroom and a 76-m (250-ft) long library, along with a series of tunnels claimed to be wide enough to drive a horse and carriage. Within the complex, food was delivered to the duke on miniature railways.

6 Brighton sewers, East Sussex

The Victorian sewers beneath Brighton comprise an extensive network of brick-lined tunnels. They are open to the public on pre-booked guided tours and have become a popular tourist attraction.

7 Post Office railway, London

A 10-km (6.5-mile) underground track between Paddington Station and Whitechapel sorting offices, it was served by a fleet of 2-ft gauge driverless electric trains, once transporting 30,000 mailbags containing four million letters and packets every day. It operated from 1927 until its closure on 30 May 2003. It features in the film *Hudson Hawk* (1991), in which it stands in for a secret Vatican railway in which Bruce Willis escapes his pursuers.

8 Cabinet War Rooms, London

Recently opened to the public, these underground emergency headquarters were used by Winston Churchill's wartime government. They consist of 24,000 sq m (258,334 sq ft) of blast-proof rooms, 10 m (40 ft) below street level. Work on their construction started in June 1938 and were completed just prior to the outbreak of the Second World War. They were closed in 1945 and in 1984 opened to the public along with a Churchill Museum.

9 Stockport Air Raid Shelters, Greater Manchester

Now open to the public, the shelters, with a network of tunnels almost 1.6 km (1 mile) long, once sheltered 6,500 people. They have been recreated to convey a precise sense of underground life during the Second World War, including the facility of a 16-seater toilet.

10 Kelvedon Hatch Secret Nuclear Bunker, Essex

Although no longer secret (it is open to the public), during the Cold War Kelvedon Hatch, fronted by an innocuous bungalow, was a subterranean bunker 38 m (125 ft) below the surface, part of Britain's air defence network known as ROTOR, capable of housing up to 600 key personnel in the event of nuclear attack.

UNUSUAL BRITISH MUSEUMS

1 **Museum of Brands, Packaging and Advertising, Notting Hill, London**
Housing the Robert Opie collection, the world's largest collection of packaging and related materials.

2 **Colman's Mustard Shop & Museum, Norwich**
The museum of the history of mustard.

3 **Cumberland Pencil Museum, Keswick**
Located in the area where graphite was first mined for pencils and the first pencil factory built in 1832.

4 **Dog Collar Museum, Leeds Castle, Maidstone**
A collection of dog collars, mostly dating from the Middle Ages (no dogs admitted).

5 **Jack Hampshire Pram Museum, Pailton, Rugby**
A collection of vintage baby carriages.

6 **Lawnmower Museum, Trerice**
The Lawnmower Museum is in the grounds of Trerice House, a National Trust property. (Another, the British Lawnmower Museum, is in Southport.)

7 **Lock Museum, Willenhall, West Midlands**
Locks, keys and lock-making tools displayed in a Victorian locksmith's house.

8 **Museum of Mental Health, Fieldhead Hospital, Wakefield**
Part of the Stephen Beaumont Museum, it includes a padded cell and other exhibits from the West Riding Pauper Lunatic Asylum, built in 1818.

9 **Verdant Works, Dundee**
A collection that explores the history of jute.

10 **Museum of Witchcraft, Boscastle, Cornwall**
Founded in 1951, it claims to be the world's largest collection devoted to witchcraft.

A NATION
OF ANIMAL
LOVERS

LARGEST NATIVE LAND MAMMALS in the UK

Mammal	Maximum length
1 Red deer (*Cervus elaphus*)	240 cm (94 in)
2 Roe deer (*Capreolus capreolus*)	135 cm (53 in)
3 Wild cat (*Felis silvestris silvestris*)	130 cm (51 in)
4 Red fox (*Vulpes vulpes*)	120 cm (47 in)
5= Badger (*Meles meles*)	80 cm (31 in)
= European otter (*Lutra lutra*)	80 cm (31 in)
7 Brown hare (*Lepus europaeus*)	70 cm (28 in)
8 Pine marten (*Martes martes*)	50 cm (20 in)
9 European polecat (*Mustela putorius*)	44 cm (17 in)
10 Stoat (*Mustela erminea*)	30 cm (12 in)

This list is restricted to species that are believed to have lived in the British Isles since ancient times, excluding domesticated species such as sheep, pigs, rabbits, cattle and horses that arrived with the Romans, Vikings or Normans. The grey squirrel is a relatively recent introduction, while the beaver, which became extinct in the 17th century, was reintroduced experimentally in 2005.

INVASIVE ANIMAL SPECIES
in the UK

1   **American bullfrog** (*Rana catesbeiana*)
Small colonies of these predatory creatures have been discovered in southern England and thus far have been controlled, so they are not yet considered a serious threat.

2   **American mink** (*Mustela vison*)
Mink were introduced in England for fur farming in 1929. Escapees have been breeding in the wild throughout Britain, where they destroy birds' eggs.

3   **Chinese mitten crab** (*Eriocheir sinensis*)
This East Asian species has been found in the Thames, Humber and Medway, where it is a threat to native crayfish populations.

4   **Citrus longhorn beetle** (*Anoplophora chinensis*)
A recent arrival in the UK, this Asian beetle is causing damage to native British tree species.

5   **Grey squirrel** (*Sciurus carolinensis*)
One of the best-known invaders, grey squirrels have ousted the indigenous red squirrels.

6   **Harlequin ladybird** (*Harmonia axyridis*)
Found in Britain since the summer of 2004 and now widespread in southern England, these ladybirds compete with native species.

7   **New Zealand flatworm** (*Arthurdendyus triangulatus*)
Believed to have arrived in the UK with imported plants in the 1960s, the species is especially prevalent in Scotland, where it destroys the native earthworm population.

8   **Ruddy duck** (*Oxyura jamaicensis*)
The UK is now host to 95 per cent of the entire European population of this species, which was introduced from North and Central America in the 1950s.

9   **Signal crayfish** (*Pacifastacus leniusculus*)
One of several invasive species of crayfish in the UK, they spread disease among native crayfish, destroy plants and invertebrates and cause environmental damage.

10 **Slipper limpet** (*Crepidula fornicata*)
A North American invader, the species damages native oysters.

Source: GB Non-native Species Secretariat
A recent audit estimated that there were 2,721 non-native species of animals and plants in the UK, of which these are among the most invasive.

MOST COMMON BRITISH BIRDS

	Bird	Estimated maximum number breeding in the UK*
1	Wren (*Troglodytes troglodytes*)	8,512,000
2	Common chaffinch (*Fringilla coelebs*)	5,974,000
3	Robin (*Erithacus rubecula*)	5,895,000
4	Blackbird (*Turdus merula*)	4,935,000
5	House sparrow (*Passer domesticus*)	3,675,000
6	Blue tit (*Cyanistes caeruleus*)	3,535,000
7	Wood pigeon (*Columba palumbus*)	3,160,000
8	Willow warbler (*Phylloscopus trochilus*)	2,125,000
9	Northern lapwing (*Vanellus vanellus*)	2,100,000
10	Great tit (*Parus major*)	2,074,000

* Ranked by upper estimate
Source: Helen Baker, *et al*, *Population Estimates of Birds in Great Britain and the United Kingdom*, 2006
Vera Lynn's popular Second World War anthem proclaimed that 'There'll be Bluebirds over the White Cliffs of Dover', but there won't. Perhaps unbeknown to the song's US composers, Walter Kent and Nat Burton, the bluebird is indigenous to the Americas and never visits Britain.

RAREST BRITISH BIRDS

Bird	Estimated number of breeding pairs in the UK
1= Black-winged stilt (*Himantopus himantopus*)	0–1
= Bluethroat (*Luscinia svecica*)	0–1
= Great reed warbler (*Acrocephalus scirpaceus*)	0–1
= Iberian chiffchaff (*Phylloscopus ibericus*)	0–1
= Icterine warbler (*Hippolais icterina*)	0–1
= Savi's warbler (*Locustella luscinioides*)	0–1
= Wryneck (*Jynx torquilla*)	0–1
8 Brambling (*Fringilla montifringilla*)	0–2
9= Common rosefinch (*Carpodacus erythrinus*)	0–4
= Eurasian spoonbill (*Platalea leucorodia*)	0–4

Source: Helen Baker, *et al*, *Population Estimates of Birds in Great Britain and the United Kingdom*, 2006
All these birds are endangered in that there are estimated to be between none or at most four breeding pairs of the species. The red-backed shrike (*Lanius collurio*) is similarly endangered, with only 0–5 pairs.

10
FAMOUS PRESERVED BRITISH ANIMALS ·

1 Parrot
A grey parrot dating from 1702, displayed in Westminster Abbey with a wax effigy of its owner, Frances Stewart, Duchess of Richmond and Lennox, is believed to be the oldest example of taxidermy in Britain.

2 Eclipse
The racehorse Eclipse took his name from a solar eclipse at the time of his birth, 1 April 1764. He won every race by such a huge margin that owners refused to race their horses against him. He retired to stud (as much as 95 per cent of today's thoroughbreds are thought to contain Eclipse DNA) and died in 1789. In an attempt to discover the secret of his speed, his body was studied, laying the foundations for veterinary medicine in Britain. His skeleton is displayed at the Royal Veterinary College, Hawkshead, Hertfordshire.

3 Athena
The pet owl that nurse Florence Nightingale acquired in Athens, Greece, died in 1855 and is preserved in the Florence Nightingale Museum at St Thomas's Hospital, London.

4 London Jack
From 1894 to 1900 a dog called London Jack carried a box at Paddington Station, London, one of several that collected money for the families of railwaymen killed at work. After his death, Jack's body was preserved and displayed in a glass case until 1921. It is now at the Natural History Museum, Tring, Hertfordshire, with over 80 other notable dogs.

5 Sparrow
The bird is believed to have been killed by a ball bowled by Jehangir Khan for Cambridge University in a match against the MCC at Lord's Cricket Ground on 3 July 1936. It was stuffed and mounted on the ball that killed it and is now displayed in the MCC Museum, where it is seen by some 50,000 visitors a year.

6 Mick the Miller
Considered greyhound racing's greatest champion, Mick the Miller won five classic races in his brief career (1929–31) and was the first dog to win the English Derby twice. After his death in 1939, Mick was mounted and displayed at the Natural History Museum, London, before being transferred to Tring.

7 Chi Chi
The giant panda Chi Chi was one of the most popular animals at London Zoo, where she lived from 5 September 1958 to 22 July 1972. Her body, stuffed by taxidermist Roy Hale, has since been displayed at the Natural History Museum. The WWF panda symbol was based on drawings of Chi Chi by naturalist Gerald Watterson.

8 Guy the Gorilla

Guy arrived at London Zoo on Guy Fawkes Day, 5 November 1947, hence his name. He died there on 8 June 1978 and was stuffed by taxidermist Arthur Hayward at the Natural History Museum, where he remains.

9 Dolly

Dolly the sheep, the world's first cloned mammal, was born on 5 July 1996 at the Roslin Institute, Edinburgh, and named after the country and western singer Dolly Parton. Since Dolly's death on 14 February 2002, her body has been exhibited by the Royal Museum of Scotland.

10 Thames whale

In January 2006 a 5-m (16-ft), 7-tonne female northern bottlenose whale was discovered in the Thames in central London. She attracted huge crowds and received extensive TV and press coverage as attempts were made to rescue her, but she died. Her skeleton was recovered and since 2007 has been displayed in London, first at the Guardian and Observer Archive and Visitor Centre and now at the Natural History Museum.

Taxidermy, the technique of mounting animals for display, began in the 18th century as a way of preserving sporting trophies and specimens collected by naturalists for museums. The Natural History Museum in London has one of the world's largest collections, with an outpost at Tring, created by naturalist Lord Rothschild. Other major British collections open to the public include the Oxford University Museum of Natural History and the Booth Museum of Natural History, Brighton, which includes tableaux by Walter Potter (1835–1918), such as 'Who Killed Cock Robin?', in which stuffed animals enact the verse.

OLDEST ZOOS
in the UK

	Zoo	Opened
1	London Zoo (opened to public 1847)	27 Apr 1828
2	Bristol Zoo	11 Jul 1836
3	Edinburgh Zoo	22 Jul 1913
4	Paignton Zoo (formerly Primley Zoological Gardens)	19 Jul 1923
5	ZSL Whipsnade Zoo	23 May 1931
6	Chester Zoo	10 Jun 1931
7	Chessington Zoo (now part of Chessington World of Adventures)	28 Jul 1931
8	Belfast Zoo (formerly Bellevue)	10 Mar 1934
9	Dudley Zoo	18 May 1937
10	Jersey Zoological Park	26 Mar 1959

The menagerie at the Tower of London may have been established as early as the 13th century and was opened to the public in the 18th, but once London Zoo opened, the animals were transferred there. Belle Vue Zoo, Manchester, was opened in 1836, but closed in 1977, and Glasgow, opened in 1947 and closed in 2003.

TYPES OF PET
in the UK

	Pet	Population
1	Dogs	7,300,000
2	Cats	7,200,000
3	Rabbits	1,400,000
4	Birds	800,000
5	Hamsters	500,000
6	Horses and ponies	300,000
7	Snakes	200,000
8	Gerbils	140,000
9	Tortoises and turtles	120,000
10	Rats	100,000

Source: Pet Food Manufacturers' Association
An estimated 43 per cent of UK households – 11,200,000 – own a pet. In 2007, the UK pet food market was valued at £1.7 billion, up 3 per cent from 2006.

TOP 10

CATS' NAMES
in the UK

1   Molly

2   Felix

3   Smudge

4   Sooty

5   Tigger

6   Charlie

7   Alfie

8   Oscar

9   Millie

10   Misty

Source: RSPCA survey

DOGS' NAMES
in the UK

1   Max

2   Molly

3   Sam/Sammy

4   Meg/Megan

5   Ben

6   Holly

7   Charlie

8   Oscar

9   Barney

10 Millie/Milly

Source: Oscar Pet Foods

PEDIGREE DOG BREEDS
in the UK

	Breed	Number registered by the Kennel Club (2007)
1	Labrador retriever	45,079
2	Cocker spaniel	20,883
3	English springer spaniel	14,702
4	Staffordshire bull terrier	12,167
5	German shepherd dog (Alsatian)	12,116
6	Cavalier King Charles spaniel	11,422
7	Golden retriever	9,557
8	Border terrier	8,814
9	West Highland white terrier	8,309
10	Boxer	8,191

Source: The Kennel Club

CRUFTS DOG SHOW WINNERS

	Breed	Years	Wins
1	Cocker spaniel	1930, 1931, 1938, 1939, 1948, 1950, 1996	7
2=	Irish setter	1981, 1993, 1995, 1999	4
=	Welsh terrier	1951, 1959, 1994, 1998	4
4=	Alsatian	1965, 1969, 1971	3
=	English setter	1964, 1977, 1988	3
=	Fox terrier (wire)	1962, 1975, 1978	3
=	Greyhound	1928, 1934, 1956	3
=	Poodle (standard)	1955, 1985, 2002	3
=	Labrador retriever	1932, 1933, 1937	3
10=	Afghan hound	1983, 1987	2
=	Airedale terrier	1961, 1986	2
=	Kerry blue terrier	1979, 2000	2
=	Lakeland terrier	1963, 1967	2
=	Pointer	1935, 1958	2
=	Poodle (toy)	1966, 1982	2
=	West Highland white terrier	1976, 1990	2
=	Whippet	1992, 2004	2

Source: The Kennel Club

PETS OF FAMOUS BRITONS

1 **Mathe**
Referred to in 1399, Richard II's favourite greyhound is one of the earliest-known named celebrity pets in Britain.

2 **Flush**
The poet Elizabeth Barrett Browning's cocker spaniel became famous as the central character in Virginia Woolf's book *Flush: A Biography* (1933).

3 **Coco**
Queen Victoria's African grey parrot was taught to sing 'God Save the Queen'.

4 **Unnamed wombat**
Among other creatures, at his Chelsea, London house, Pre-Raphaelite painter and poet Dante Gabriel Rossetti kept two laughing jackasses, kangaroos, armadillos and a racoon.

5 **Williamina**
Charles Dickens's Williamina was called William until she gave birth to a litter of kittens, one of which gained his attention by putting out candles with its paw.

6 **Foss**
Edward Lear's cat Foss was the subject of a number of his nonsense poems and comic drawings. When the cat died in 1887, Lear imaginatively claimed he was 31 years old.

7 **Luath**
Luath was the Newfoundland dog belonging to J. M. Barrie that was the model of Nana in his book (originally play) *Peter Pan* (1904).

8 **Xarifa**
Beatrix Potter kept rabbits, a hedgehog, dogs, sheep, pigs and other animals, many of which feature in her books. Xarifa, her dormouse, appears in *The Fairy Caravan* (1929).

9 **Susan**
George VI started the royal fashion for corgis with Rozavel Golden Eagle (Dookie), in 1933. Queen Elizabeth's first corgi, Susan, was given to her on her 18th birthday in 1944.

10 **Margate**
The cat turned up at 10 Downing Street and was adopted by Churchill on 10 October 1953, the day of an important speech at Margate, hence its name. Subsequent feline occupants of No. 10 have included Peter, Harold Wilson's Siamese cat Nemo, Mrs Thatcher's Wilberforce, Humphrey (named after Sir Humphrey Appleby in *Yes Minister*) and Sybil.

RULE,
BRITANNIA!

IN LINE TO THE BRITISH THRONE

1   **HRH The Prince of Wales**
    Prince Charles Philip Arthur George (b. 14 Nov 1948) – *then his elder son…*

2   **HRH Prince William of Wales**
    Prince William Arthur Philip Louis (b. 21 Jun 1982) – *then his younger brother…*

3   **HRH Prince Henry ('Harry') of Wales**
    Prince Henry Charles Albert David (b. 15 Sep 1984) – *then his uncle…*

4   **HRH The Duke of York**
    Prince Andrew Albert Christian Edward (b. 19 Feb 1960) – *then his elder daughter…*

5   **HRH Princess Beatrice of York**
    Princess Beatrice Elizabeth Mary (b. 8 Aug 1988) – *then her younger sister…*

6   **HRH Princess Eugenie of York**
    Princess Eugenie Victoria Helena (b. 23 Mar 1990) – *then her uncle…*

7   **HRH Prince Edward**
    Prince Edward Antony Richard Louis (b. 10 Mar 1964) – *then his son…*

8   **Viscount Severn**
    James Alexander Philip Theo Windsor (b. 17 Dec 2007) – *then his sister…*

9   **Lady Louise Windsor**
    Louise Alice Elizabeth Mary Mountbatten Windsor (b. 8 Nov 2003) – *then her aunt…*

10 **HRH The Princess Royal**
    Princess Anne Elizabeth Alice Louise (b. 15 Aug 1950)

In the past decade, the order of succession has altered, first with the birth in 1988 of Princess Beatrice, ousting David Albert Charles Armstrong-Jones, Viscount Linley (b. 3 November 1961), from the No. 10 position, while the birth in 1990 of her sister, Princess Eugenie, evicted HRH Princess Margaret. The birth of Lady Louise Windsor meant that Zara Phillips fell out of the Top 10, and that of Viscount Severn pushed Peter Phillips into 11th place.

BUSIEST MEMBERS OF THE ROYAL FAMILY

	Member	Official engagements (2007)*
1	Princess Royal	462
2	Prince of Wales	409
3	The Queen	393
4	Duke of Edinburgh	334
5	Duke of York	264
6	Duke of Gloucester	227
7	Earl of Wessex	223
8	Duke of Kent	178
9	Countess of Wessex	139
10=	Duchess of Cornwall	125
=	Duchess of Gloucester	125

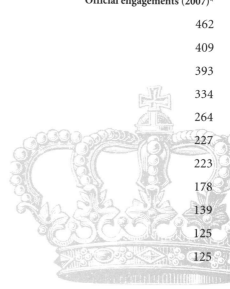

* Domestic total

Source: Tim O'Donovan

In addition to those engagements carried out in the UK in 2007, members of the royal family conducted many additional engagements abroad, with Prince Andrew, Duke of York, leading the field with a total of 292. During the year, their military commitments curtailed the official engagements of Princes William and Harry, who logged 16 and 12 respectively. Tim O'Donovan, who has been compiling this list for many years, points out that it should not be interpreted as a 'league table' of royal performance, since it takes no account of the respective time and effort demanded by each engagement.

LONGEST-LIVED BRITISH MONARCHS

	Monarch	Born	Died	Years	Lifespan Months	Days
1	Elizabeth II	21 Apr 1926	–	82	7	11*
2	Victoria	24 May 1819	22 Jan 1901	81	7	29
3	George III	4 Jun 1738	29 Jan 1820	81	7	25
4	Edward VIII	23 Jun 1894	28 May 1972	77	11	5
5	George II	10 Nov 1683	25 Oct 1760	76	11	15
6	William IV	21 Aug 1765	20 Jun 1837	71	9	30
7	George V	3 Jun 1865	20 Jan 1936	70	7	17
8	Elizabeth I	7 Sep 1533	24 Mar 1603	69	6	17
9	Edward VII	9 Nov 1841	6 May 1910	68	5	27
10	Edward I	17 Jun 1239	7 Jul 1307	68	0	20

* Age on 1 January 2009

As runners-up to Queen Elizabeth II, Queen Victoria and George III are close rivals, and George's dates might suggest that he lived slightly longer than Victoria. However, during his lifetime, in 1752, the Gregorian calendar was adopted in Great Britain, as a result of which 11 days were lost. Taking this into account, Queen Victoria lived four days longer than George III.

SHORTEST-LIVED BRITISH MONARCHS

	Monarch	Born	Died	Lifespan Years	Months	Days
1	Edward V	2 Nov 1470	c.1483*	12	–	–
2	Edward VI	12 Oct 1537	6 Jul 1553	15	8	24
3	Jane	c.1536/7*	12 Feb 1554	16	–	–
4	Mary II	30 Apr 1662	28 Dec 1694	32	7	28
5	Richard III	2 Oct 1452	22 Aug 1485	32	10	20
6	Richard II	6 Jan 1367	14 Feb 1400	33	1	8
7	Henry V	16 Sep 1386*	31 Aug 1422	35	11	15
8	William II	c.1060*	2 Aug 1100	40	–	–
9	Edward IV	28 Apr 1442	9 Apr 1483	40	11	12
10	Richard I	8 Sep 1157	6 Apr 1199	41	6	29

* Precise date uncertain, hence age approximate

LONGEST-REIGNING BRITISH MONARCHS

	Monarch	Reign	Years	Duration Months	Days
1	Victoria	20 Jun 1837–22 Jan 1901	63	7	2
2	George III	25 Oct 1760–29 Jan 1820	59	3	4
3	Elizabeth II	6 Feb 1952–	57	–	–*
4	Henry III	18 Oct 1216–16 Nov 1272	56	0	29
5	Edward III	25 Jan 1327–21 Jun 1377	50	4	27
6	Elizabeth I	17 Nov 1558–24 Mar 1603	44	4	7
7	Henry VI	31 Aug 1422–4 Mar 1461; 31 Oct 1470–11 Apr 1471	38	11	15
8	Henry VIII	22 Apr 1509–28 Jan 1547	37	9	6
9	Charles II	30 Jan 1649–3 Sep 1651;† 29 May 1660–6 Feb 1685	36	7	0
10	Henry I	2 Aug 1100–1 Dec 1135	35	3	29

* As at 6 February 2009
† Reign in Scotland; discounting 1649–60 Interregnum

SHORTEST-REIGNING BRITISH MONARCHS

	Monarch	Reign	Years	Duration Months	Days
1	Jane	10–19 Jul 1553	–	–	9
2	Edward V	9 Apr–25 Jun 1483	–	–	77
3	Edward VIII	20 Jan–11 Dec 1936	–	10	21
4	Richard III	20 Jun 1483–22 Aug 1485	2	2	2
5	James II	6 Feb 1685–11 Dec 1688	3	10	5
6	Mary I	19 Jul 1553–17 Nov 1558	5	3	29
7	Mary II	13 Feb 1689–28 Dec 1694	5	10	15
8	Edward VI	28 Jan 1547–6 Jul 1553	6	5	8
9	William IV	26 Jun 1830–20 Jun 1837	7	11	25
10	Edward VII	22 Jan 1901–6 May 1910	9	3	14

Queen Jane, Lady Jane Grey, ruled fleetingly, before being sent to the Tower of London, where she was executed the following year. Edward V was one of the 'Princes in the Tower', allegedly murdered on the orders of their uncle, Richard III. Edward VIII made his famous radio abdication speech on 11 December 1936, before his coronation.

THE 10
LAST BRITISH MONARCHS TO DIE VIOLENTLY

	Monarch	Cause*	Date
1	William III	Riding accident	8 Mar 1702
2	Charles I	Beheaded	30 Jan 1649
3	Jane	Beheaded	12 Feb 1554
4	Richard III	In battle	22 Aug 1485
5	Edward V	Murdered	1483†
6	Henry VI	Murdered	21 May 1471
7	Edward II	Murdered	21 Sep 1327
8	Richard I	Arrow wound	6 Apr 1199
9	William II	Arrow wound	2 Aug 1100
10	William I	Riding accident	9 Sep 1087

* Including illnesses resulting from injuries
† Precise date unknown

William III died of pneumonia contracted after breaking his collarbone in a fall from his horse, Sorrel, which stumbled on a molehill at Hampton Court on 21 February 1702. This gave rise to the celebrated Jacobite toast to the mole that indirectly caused William's death, 'the little gentleman in the black velvet waistcoat'.

LAST SCOTTISH MONARCHS

	Monarch	Rule
1	Anne	1702–7
2	William II	1689–1702
3	Mary II	1689–94
4	James VII (II of England)	1685–9
5	Charles II	1649–85
6	Charles I	1625–49*
7	James VI (I of England)	1567–1625
8	Mary I (Queen of Scots)	1542–67*
9	James V	1513–42
10	James IV	1488–1513†

* Executed
† Killed at the Battle of Flodden Field
Since the Act of Union of 1 May 1707, all monarchs have ruled both England and Scotland.

BRITISH ROYAL NICKNAMES

1 ### Brandy Nan
Queen Anne was so called because of her alleged taste for fine French brandy. She was also known as Mrs Bull and Mrs Morley.

2 ### Brenda
Queen Elizabeth II's nickname, according to *Private Eye*. In the same publication the Duke of Edinburgh is Keith and Prince Charles Brian.

3 ### Farmer George
George III gained his nickname from his interest in agriculture.

4 ### The Merry Monarch
Party-loving Charles II was also known as the Mutton Eating Monarch and Old Rowley (after a stallion in his stables).

5 ### Prince of Whales
George IV was also known as the Beau of Princes, Prince Florizel, Prinny, Admiral George Carlton, Fum the Fourth and the First Gentleman of Europe.

6 ### Richard Crookback
There was no evidence that Richard III was deformed, his title probably deriving from Shakespeare's portrayal of him. He was also called 'the Hogge' – although William Collingbourne, who coined the epithet in a poem, was executed for it.

7 ### Silly Billy
The nickname of William IV, also known as the Sailor King, derived from his visit to Bedlam lunatic asylum, where an inmate shouted it at him.

8 ### Virgin Queen
Elizabeth I collected numerous nicknames during her long reign, including Astraea, Belphoebe, Gloriana, Good Queen Bess, the Fairie Queene, the Peerless Oriana, the Queen of the Sea, the Queen of Shepherds, the World's Wonder and the Untamed Heifer.

9 ### The Widow of Windsor
Victoria's nickname featured in a poem of 1890 by Rudyard Kipling. She was also known as Mrs Brown, Mrs Melbourne, the Famine Queen and the Grandmother of Europe.

10 ### The Wisest Fool in Christendom
James I was so called, as well as the Solomon of England, Scottish Jimmy, the Second (or Scottish) Solomon, a Royal Fool and Queen James.

BRITISH CROWN JEWELS

1 ## Imperial State Crown
Made for the coronation of George VI in 1937, the crown contains 2,868 diamonds as well as pearls and other precious stones, including the Black Prince's Ruby, which Henry V wore at the Battle of Agincourt in 1415.

2 ## Sovereign's Orb
Made for the coronation of Charles II in 1661, it is a hollow gold sphere with a band of jewels and a cross symbolizing the monarch's role as Defender of the Faith.

3 ## Sceptre with the Cross
Also known as St Edward's Sceptre, it was made for Charles II in 1661. The 530.20-carat Great Star of Africa, the second largest diamond in the world, was cut from the Cullinan and added in 1905. In the coronation ceremony, it is held in the monarch's right hand.

4 ## Sceptre with the Dove
In the coronation, the gold and jewel-encrusted Sceptre with the Dove is held in the monarch's left hand.

5 ## St Edward's Crown
Made in 1661, the heavy gold crown with 444 precious stones is the model on which all later crowns and the symbol on the Royal Coat of Arms have been based.

6 ## Ampulla
Believed to date from the reign of Henry IV, the Ampulla, or eagle of gold, contains the oil used to anoint the sovereign during the coronation.

7 ## Anointing Spoon
Dating from the late 12th century, it was restored for the coronation of Charles II.

8 ## Crown of Scotland
Remade from an older crown for James V of Scotland in 1540, the gold crown, the oldest in Britain, is kept in Edinburgh Castle with other Scottish Crown Jewels.

9 ## Great Sword of State
The largest of several swords in the Crown Jewels, it is carried in front of the monarch by the Lord Great Chamberlain at coronations and the State Opening of Parliament.

10 ## Queen Mother's Crown
Made for Elizabeth for the coronation of George VI in 1937, with the 105-carat Koh-i-Noor diamond set in it, the crown was placed on her coffin at her funeral in 2002.

TOP 10

OLDEST DUKEDOMS
in Britain

	Dukedom	Current holder	Title created
1	Norfolk	18th	28 Jun 1483
2	Somerset	19th	16 Feb 1547
3	Hamilton	15th	12 Apr 1643
4	Buccleuch	10th	20 Apr 1663
5	Richmond (Lennox & Gordon)	10th	9 Aug 1675
6	Grafton	11th	11 Sep 1675
7	Beaufort	11th	2 Dec 1682
8	St Albans	14th	10 Jan 1684
9	Bedford	15th	11 May 1694
10	Devonshire	12th	12 May 1694

This list excludes royal dukes, which are titles that are conferred on members of the royal family, rather than inherited. Britain's current royal dukes are Edinburgh – Prince Philip; Cornwall (England) and Rothesay (Scotland) – Prince Charles; York – Prince Andrew; Gloucester – Prince Richard; and Kent – Prince Edward.

UNUSUAL BRITISH TITLES

1   **Bluemantle Pursuivant of Arms in Ordinary**
    One of several officers in the College of Arms, dating back to the 15th century.

2   **Gentleman Usher of the Black Rod**
    As part of his ceremonial duties, Black Rod is the officer who has a door slammed in his face during the State Opening of Parliament and bangs on it three times with his ebony rod to request admittance by the monarch.

3   **Gold Stick**
    A bodyguard to the monarch, who carries a long gold stick. One of the holders of the title is the Colonel of the Blues and Royals – Princess Anne is the present incumbent.

4   **Lord of the Isles**
    A Scottish feudal title, since James V held by the eldest male child of the monarch, hence currently held by Prince Charles.

5   **Lord Warden of the Cinque Ports**
    The leading officer in the group of five important British ports, Hastings, New Romney, Hythe, Dover and Sandwich, the role dates back to the 12th century.

6   **Marker of the Swans**
    The title was created in 1993 when the Keeper of the King's Swans' role was split into this and a Warden of the Swans. Paradoxically, during the annual swan-upping, the Marker of the Swans does not mark them.

7   **President of Tynwald**
    The presiding officer of the High Court of Tynwald, the legislature of the Isle of Man. Other titles include The First Deemster and Clerk of the Rolls.

8   **Renter Warden**
    An officer in a City of London livery company. The head of a company is the Master, while other officials include an Upper Warden and Beadle.

9   **Seigneur of Sark**
    The leading officer in the legislature of the Channel Island of Sark. A female incumbent is called the Dame of Sark.

10 **Water Bailiff**
    A legal officer appointed to police bodies of water, including fishing activities. They have the power of stop and search and arrest.

LONGEST-SERVING BRITISH PRIME MINISTERS

TOP 10

Prime minister	Total duration		
	Years	Months	Days
1 Sir Robert Walpole Period in office: 3 Apr 1721–8 Feb 1742	20	10	5
2 William Pitt the Younger, Periods in office: 19 Dec 1783–14 Mar 1801; 10 May 1804–23 Jan 1806	18	11	8
3 Earl of Liverpool Period in office: 7 Jun 1812–17 Feb 1827	14	8	10
4 Marquess of Salisbury Periods in office: 23 Jun 1885–28 Jan 1886; 26 Jul 1886– 11 Aug 1892; 25 Jun 1895–11 Jul 1902	13	8	6
5 William Gladstone Periods in office: 4 Dec 1868–17 Feb 1874; 23 Apr 1880– 9 Jun 1885; 1 Feb 1886–20 Jul 1886 and 15 Aug 1892–2 Mar 1894	12	4	3
6 Lord North Period in office: 28 Jan 1770–20 Mar 1782	12	1	20
7 Margaret Thatcher Period in office: 4 May 1979–29 Nov 1990	11	6	25
8 Henry Pelham Period in office: 27 Aug 1743–6 Mar 1754	10	6	7
9 Tony Blair Period in office: 2 May 1997–27 Jun 2007	10	1	25
10 Viscount Palmerston Periods in office: 6 Feb 1855–21 Feb 1858; 12 Jun 1859–18 Oct 1865	9	4	24

Sir Robert Walpole is regarded as the first British prime minister, although the office was not officially recognized until 1905, most earlier prime ministers deriving their authority from their position as First Lord of the Treasury.

ZODIAC SIGNS OF BRITISH PRIME MINISTERS

Sign	PMs
1= Aries (21 Mar–20 Apr)	6
= Taurus (21 Apr–21 May)	6
= Libra (24 Sep–23 Oct)	6
4= Pisces (20 Feb–20 Mar)	5
= Gemini (22 May–22 Jun)	5
6= Aquarius (21 Jan–19 Feb)	4
= Virgo (24 Aug–23 Sep)	4
= Scorpio (24 Oct–22 Nov)	4
9= Cancer (23 Jun–23 Jul)	3
= Leo (24 Jul–23 Aug)	3
= Capricorn (22 Dec–20 Jan)	3

The birth pattern of British prime ministers shows a remarkably even spread across the 12 signs of the zodiac. Their representatives are similarly balanced across the various political parties – except for Gemini, where all five were either Tories or Conservatives, and Sagittarius (23 November–21 December), the only sign outside the Top 10, with just two PMs, Benjamin Disraeli and Winston Churchill, who were both Conservatives. The precise date of birth of the Earl of Wilmington, Whig PM from 1742 to 1743, is unknown.

THE 10

FIRST WOMEN MPS
in the UK

Name/party	Constituency	Elected
1 Constance, Countess Markievicz (Sinn Féin)	Dublin, St Patrick's	14 Dec 1918
2 Nancy, Viscountess Astor (Con.)	Plymouth, Sutton	28 Nov 1919
3 Margaret Wintringham (Lib.)	Lincolnshire, Louth	22 Sep 1921
4 Mabel Philipson (Con.)	Berwick-upon-Tweed	31 May 1923
5= Katherine, Duchess of Atholl (Con.)	Perth and Kinross	6 Dec 1923
= Rt Hon. Margaret Bondfield (Lab.)*	Northampton	6 Dec 1923
= Dorothea Jewson (Lab.)	Norwich	6 Dec 1923
= Arabella Susan Lawrence (Lab.)	East Ham, North	6 Dec 1923
= Lady Vera Terrington (Lib.)	Buckinghamshire, Wycombe	6 Dec 1923
10 Rt Hon. Ellen Wilkinson (Lab.)	Middlesbrough, East	29 Oct 1924

* First woman Cabinet minister (Minister of Labour, 1929–31)
Countess Markievicz was the first woman elected as a British Member of Parliament, but in common with other Sinn Féin members did not take her seat. American-born Nancy Astor was the first to do so, holding her seat until her retirement in 1945. Since her, some 290 women have served as MPs.

AREAS OF UK GOVERNMENT EXPENDITURE

	Department	Departmental expenditure limits (2009–10)
1	Health	£99,900,000,000
2	Children, Schools and Families	£49,200,000,000
3	Defence	£35,200,000,000
4	Local Government	£25,600,000,000
5	Scotland	£25,400,000,000
6	Innovation, Universities and Skills	£17,200,000,000
7	Wales	£13,500,000,000
8=	Home Office	£9,400,000,000
=	Justice	£9,400,000,000
10	Northern Ireland Executive	£8,400,000,000
	Top 10 total	*£293,200,000,000*
	Total estimated expenditure	*£339,200,000,000*

Source: HM Treasury

10

STRANGE BRITISH LAWS

1   Pelican touching
Under Section 23 of the London Royal and Other Parks and Gardens Regulations of 1977,
'touching a pelican' was forbidden, unless written permission was first obtained.

2   Scotsmen shooting
In the city of York it is legal to murder a Scotsman within the ancient city walls with a bow
and arrow, except on Sundays.

3   Armour wearing
Since 1313 it has been forbidden for Members of Parliament to wear suits of armour in the
House of Commons. It is also illegal to die in the Houses of Parliament.

4   Pensioner impersonating
It is illegal to impersonate a Chelsea Pensioner.

5   Mince pie eating
Oliver Cromwell's parliament passed a law banning the eating of mince pies on Christmas
Day.

6   Stamp inverting
It is an act of treason to place a postage stamp bearing the British monarch upside down.

7   Sheep driving
Freemen of the City of London are allowed to drive a flock of sheep across London Bridge
without paying a toll and are permitted to drive geese down Cheapside.

8   Topless retailing
In Liverpool, it is illegal for a woman to be topless unless she works in a tropical fish store.

9   Whale distributing
The head of any dead whale found on the British coast automatically becomes the property
of the king. By tradition, its tail went to the queen to provide whalebone for her corsets –
uselessly, since the baleen used in corsetry actually comes from the head.

10 Straw carrying
Until 1976, London taxi drivers had to carry a bale of straw in their cabs, to feed their horse,
but they were forbidden from carrying rabid dogs, people with the plague or corpses.

GREAT
BRITISH
PASTIMES

SUMMER OLYMPIC SPORTS IN WHICH THE UK has won most gold medals

	Sport	Gold medals
1	Track and field	55
2	Sailing	27
3	Rowing	24
4=	Cycling	20
=	Swimming and diving	20
6	Lawn tennis	17
7=	Shooting	14
=	Boxing	14
9	Equestrianism	6
10=	Hockey	3
=	Polo	3
=	Soccer	3
=	Wrestling	3

This takes into account all events – that is, even those that have been discontinued and the 1906 Intercalated Games – up to and including the 2008 Beijing Games. Following the UK's success in Beijing, cycling moved from 8th to joint 4th in the list.

LARGEST SPORTS STADIUMS
in the UK

	Stadium	Location	Capacity
1	Wembley Stadium	London	90,000
2	Twickenham	London	82,000
3	Old Trafford	Manchester	76,212
4	Millennium Stadium	Cardiff	74,500
5	Murrayfield Stadium	Edinburgh	67,800
6	Celtic Park	Glasgow	60,832
7	Emirates Stadium	London	60,355
8	St James's Park	Newcastle upon Tyne	52,387
9	Hampden Park	Glasgow	52,103
10	Ibrox Stadium	Glasgow	51,082

ENGLISH WICKET-TAKERS IN TEST CRICKET*

	Player	Years	Matches	Wickets
1	Ian Botham	1977–92	102	383
2	Bob Willis	1971–84	90	325
3	Fred Trueman	1952–65	67	307
4	Derek Underwood	1966–82	86	297
5	Brian Statham	1951–65	70	252
6	Matthew Hoggard	2000–08	67	248
7	Alec Bedser	1946–55	51	236
8	Andy Caddick	1993–2003	62	234
9	Darren Gough	1994–2003	58	229
10	Steve Harmison	2002–08	57	212

* As at 1 November 2008

WAYS OF BEING OUT IN CRICKET

1   Caught

2   Bowled

3   Leg before wicket

4   Run out

5   Stumped

6   Hit wicket

7   Handled the ball

8   Hit the ball twice

9   Obstructing the field

10   Timed out

The most common form of dismissal is caught. A further, but rarely used, method of being out is covered by Law 2: 'If a batsman retires because of illness, injury or any other unavoidable cause, he is entitled to resume his innings ... if for any reason he does not resume his innings it is to be recorded as Retired "out".'

OLDEST FOOTBALL LEAGUE CLUBS

	Club	Year formed
1	Notts County	1862
2	Stoke City	1863
3	Nottingham Forest	1865
4	Chesterfield	1866
5	Sheffield Wednesday	1867
6	Reading	1871
7	Wrexham	1873
8	Aston Villa	(Mar) 1874
9	Bolton Wanderers	(Jul) 1874
10	Birmingham City	1875

Birmingham City dates its origin to September 1875, slightly before Blackburn Rovers, which started in November of that year. Scotland's oldest club is Queen's Park, formed in 1867 – they remain the only amateur team in League soccer in Scotland or England. The oldest football club in the world still playing is Sheffield FC, which was formed on 24 October 1857.

FIRST £1 MILLION FOOTBALLERS
in Britain

	Player	Fee
1	**Trevor Francis** Moved from Birmingham City to Nottingham Forest in Feb 1979	£1,150,000
2	**Steve Daley** Moved from Wolverhampton Wanderers to Manchester City in Sep 1979	£1,450,000
3	**Andy Gray** Moved from Aston Villa to Wolverhampton Wanderers in Sep 1979	£1,470,000
4	**Kevin Reeves** Moved from Norwich City to Manchester City in Mar 1980	£1,000,000
5	**Clive Allen** Moved from Queen's Park Rangers to Arsenal in Jun 1980	£1,200,000
6	**Ian Wallace** Moved from Coventry City to Nottingham Forest in Jul 1980	£1,250,000
7=	**Clive Allen** Moved from Arsenal to Crystal Palace in Aug 1980	£1,250,000
=	**Kenny Sansom** Moved from Crystal Palace to Arsenal in Aug 1980	£1,350,000
9	**Garry Birtles** Moved from Nottingham Forest to Manchester United in Oct 1980	£1,250,000
10	**Justin Fashanu** Moved from Norwich City to Nottingham Forest in Aug 1981	£1,000,000

The first British player to be involved in a £2,000,000 transfer was Mark Hughes, when he went from Manchester United to Barcelona in May 1986. The first £2,000,000 transfer between British clubs was in July 1988, when Paul Gascoigne joined Spurs from Newcastle. Rangers were the first Scottish club to pay over £1,000,000 for a player when they acquired Richard Gough from Spurs for £1,500,000 in October 1987. When Ian Ferguson moved from St Mirren to Rangers in February 1988, he became the first seven-figure player to move between Scottish clubs.

TOP 10 SPORTS SINGLES
in the UK

	Title	Artist/team	Year
1	'Three Lions (The Official Song of the England Football Squad)'	Baddiel & Skinner and the Lightning Seeds	1996
2	'Three Lions 98'	Baddiel & Skinner and the Lightning Seeds	1998
3	'Back Home'	England World Cup Squad	1970
4	'World in Motion'	England World Cup Squad with New Order	1990
5	'This Time We'll Get It Right'	England World Cup Squad	1982
6	'Come On You Reds'	Manchester United Football Team	1994
7	'Move Move Move (The Red Tribe)'	Manchester Football Cup Squad	1996
8	'Sing Up For The Champions'	Reds United	1997
9	'Anfield Rap (Red Machine in Full Effect)'	Liverpool FC	1988
10	'(How Does It Feel to Be) On Top of The World'	England United	1998

All these singles made the UK Top 10, and the first four were chart-topping hits. Six were World Cup songs, three Manchester United from the 1990s and a sole representation by Liverpool.

MOST APPEARANCES BY BRITISH
PLAYERS in international rugby[*]

	Player	Country	Years	Total caps†
1	Jason Leonard	England/Lions	1990–2004	119(5)
2	Gareth Thomas	Wales/Lions	1995–2007	103(3)
3	Colin Charvis	Wales/Lions	1996–2007	96(2)
4=	Martin Johnson	England/Lions	1993–2003	92(8)
=	Gareth Llewellyn	Wales	1989–2004	92
6=	Neil Jenkins	Wales/Lions	1991–2002	91(4)
=	Malcolm O'Kelly	Ireland	1997–2008	91
=	Rory Underwood	England/Lions	1984–96	91(5)
9	Brian O'Driscoll	Ireland/Lions	1999–2008	89(4)
10=	Lawrence Dallaglio	England/Lions	1995–2007	88(3)
=	Chris Paterson	Scotland	1999–2008	88

* As at 28 July 2008
† Figures in brackets indicate the number of appearances for the British and Irish Lions

FAMOUS BRITISH RACEHORSES

1   **Arkle**
Foaled in Ireland in 1957, owned by the Duchess of Westminster and trained by Tom Dreaper, Arkle can rightly claim to be the greatest steeplechaser of all time. He competed in three Cheltenham Gold Cups (1964, 1965 and 1966) and won all three. He died on 31 May 1970.

2   **Brigadier Gerard**
The Dick Hern-trained Brigadier Gerard won 17 races from 18 starts, including 15 consecutively in 1971–2. His greatest win was perhaps in the 1971 2,000 Guineas, when he devastated Mill Reef with his pace, winning by three lengths. Over a mile he was unbeatable if the going was right.

3   **Dancing Brave**
The American-bred Dancing Brave proved his worth when he won the 1986 Prix de l'Arc de Triomphe against one of the strongest fields ever assembled in Europe, jockey Pat Eddery describing him as 'one of the best horses of all time'. Dancing Brave is perhaps best remembered for the race he failed to win, the 1986 Epsom Derby, when he finished second to Shahrastani.

4   **Desert Orchid**
The grey Desert Orchid, or simply 'Dessie' to his thousands of fans, was foaled in April 1979 and went on to become one of the best-loved horses of modern times. Trained by David Elsworth, Dessie won 34 of his 70 races, including the Irish Grand National, Cheltenham Gold Cup, Whitbread Gold Cup and the King George VI Chase on four occasions.

5   **Eclipse**
While the likes of Nijinsky, Mill Reef, Brigadier Gerard and Shergar vied for the title 'Horse of the 20th century', only one horse can claim that title for the 18th – Eclipse. In the years 1769–70 he was never beaten in 18 races and eventually retired because of lack of opposition. At stud he sired 344 foals, including three Derby winners.

6 Golden Miller

Prior to the arrival of Arkle, Golden Miller was widely regarded as the greatest chaser ever seen. He won the Cheltenham Gold Cup five years in succession (1932–36) and in 1934 completed a rare Grand National/Gold Cup double, winning the National in a then record time. Golden Miller won 28 of his 52 races.

7 Mill Reef

Bred in Virginia, USA, and foaled in 1968, Mill Reef won 12 of his 14 races between 1970 and 1972 and was second in the other two races. Victories included the Epsom Derby, the King George VI and Queen Elizabeth Stakes and the Prix de l'Arc de Triomphe, ridden on each occasion by Geoff Lewis.

8 Nijinsky

Vincent O'Brien-trained Nijinsky was probably the best-loved flat-racing horse British fans have known. He amazed everybody with a burst of pace in the 1970 Derby, when he responded to Lester Piggott's whip to win in the fastest time since 1936. He completed the Triple Crown in 1970 and also captured the King George VI and Queen Elizabeth Stakes.

9 Red Rum

Red Rum was foaled in 1965 and trained on the Southport sands by former local taxi driver Donald 'Ginger' McCain. He won the Aintree Grand National a record three times in 1973, 1974 and 1977 and was runner-up in 1975 and 1976. Red Rum died in 1995 and was buried close to the finishing post at Aintree.

10 Shergar

Shergar gained notoriety for all the wrong reasons, but it should never be forgotten what a quality racehorse he was. After winning the 1981 Epsom Derby by a record 10 lengths there were many who labelled him the best horse of the 20th century. Owned by the Aga Khan and trained by Michael Stoute, Shergar was kidnapped in Ireland on 9 February 1983, never to be seen again.

FIRST OFFICIALLY RATIFIED
MAXIMUM BREAKS in snooker

	Player/nationality	Date
1	Joe Davis (English) Exhibition match, Leicester Square Hall, London	22 Jan 1955
2	Rex Williams (English) Exhibition match, Prince's Hotel, Newlands, South Africa	22 Dec 1965
3	Steve Davis (English) Lada Classic, Civic Centre, Oldham	11 Jan 1982
4	Cliff Thorburn (Canadian) Embassy World Championship, Crucible Theatre, Sheffield	23 Apr 1983
5	Kirk Stevens (Canadian) Benson & Hedges Masters, Wembley Conference Centre, London	28 Jan 1984
6	Willie Thorne (English) UK Championship, Guildhall, Preston	17 Nov 1987
7	Tony Meo (English) Matchroom League, Winding Wheel Centre, Chesterfield	20 Feb 1988
8	Alain Robidoux (Canadian) European Open, Norbreck Castle Hotel, Blackpool	24 Sep 1988
9	John Rea (Scottish) Scottish Pro Championship, Marco's Leisure Centre, Glasgow	18 Feb 1989
10	Cliff Thorburn (Canadian) Matchroom League, Hawth Theatre, Crawley	8 Mar 1989

The first witnessed maximum break was in Australia on 26 September 1934, when New Zealander Murt O'Donoghue compiled a 147, but his achievement was never officially ratified. Steve Davis's maximum was the first to be recognized in tournament play and the first to be televised. A 147 made by John Spencer in the Holsten Lager Tournament at Slough in 1979 should have been the first to be seen on television, but the camera crew was at lunch at the time. There was double disappointment for Spencer because his break was never officially ratified by the Billiards and Snooker Control Council.

OLDEST GOLF CLUBS
in Britain

	Club	Year formed
1	Royal Burgess Golfing Society of Edinburgh	1735
2	Honourable Company of Edinburgh Golfers (Muirfield)	1744
3	Royal and Ancient (St Andrews)	1754
4	Bruntsfield Links Golfing Society	1761
5	Royal Blackheath	1766
6	Royal Musselburgh	1774
7	Royal Aberdeen	1780
8	Crail Golfing Society	1786
9	Glasgow Golf Club	1787
10	Burntisland Golf Club	1791

All these clubs are in Scotland with the exception of Royal Blackheath. The oldest in Northern Ireland is Royal Belfast (1881) and the Republic's oldest is Curragh, County Kildare (1883). The oldest Welsh club is Pontnewydd, Cwmbran (1875). The exact date of the formation of the Blackheath club is uncertain and some sources record that golf was played there in the 17th century by James VI of Scotland. However, it is generally accepted that the club was formed in 1766. The oldest-known golf site was established at Perth in 1502, shortly after a 45-year ban on golf was lifted by James IV of Scotland.

GREAT BRITISH RACES

1 Olney Pancake Race
The Pancake Race held on Shrove Tuesday every year in Olney, Buckinghamshire, is more than 500 years old. The current course, from the marketplace to the parish church, is 380 m (415 yards) long. The race starts at 11.55 a.m. and is open to housewives and young ladies over 18 who have lived in the village for the previous three months.

2 Doggett's Coat and Badge
Not only the oldest rowing race in the world but the oldest known sporting contest still in existence, this is named after Irish actor Thomas Doggett and first took place in 1715. It is now open to apprentice watermen on the River Thames. The race takes place in July and the winner receives a red coat with a silver badge.

3 Epsom Derby
One of the world's great horse races, the Derby was first held at Epsom in 1780 and won by Diomed, ridden by Sam Arnull. The race is named after the 12th Earl of Derby, who won the right to have it named after him following the toss of a coin with Sir Charles Bunbury. The current course measures 2.4 km (1 mile, 4 furlongs). During the war years 1915–18 and 1940–45 the race was held at Newmarket.

4 Boat Race
The annual boat race between the universities of Oxford and Cambridge takes place on the River Thames between Putney and Mortlake each spring over a 6.7-km (4-mile, 374-yard) course. It was first contested on 10 June 1829 between Hambledon Lock and Henley Bridge. The race's only dead heat occurred in 1877.

5 Aintree Grand National
First held in 1836 at Maghull, a Liverpool suburb approximately 6.2 km (4 miles) from Aintree, to where the race moved in 1839, it was originally known as the Grand Liverpool Steeplechase. The current circuit is approximately 7.2 km (4.5 miles) and the winning horse has to negotiate 30 fences.

6 Isle of Man TT Races
Because road racing was banned on British roads, the Auto Cycle Club and RAC held rehearsals for the 1906 International Cup Race on the Isle of Man. It proved so popular that the first Tourist Trophy was held on the island on 28 May 1907, being won by Charlie Collier. Racing now takes place over the 60-km (37-mile) mountain course each June.

7　Fastnet Race

One of the great offshore yachting races, this was first held in 1925. Taking place every two years, it sets off from Cowes in the Isle of Wight, goes round the Fastnet Rock and ends in Plymouth 9,730 km (608 miles) later. A severe storm hit the 1979 race, which resulted in 15 competitors losing their lives.

8　British Formula One Grand Prix

The British Grand Prix started life as the RAC Grand Prix at Brooklands in 1926. The term British Grand Prix was first used for the 1948 race at Silverstone. It has its place in Formula One history as it was, on 13 May 1950, the first race in the World Championship for Drivers, with Giuseppe Farina (Italy) winning the inaugural event.

9　Emsley Carr Mile

Established in 1953 to encourage runners to break the 4-minute barrier for the mile, it was first won by Gordon Pirie in a time of 4 minutes and 06.8 seconds. The winner is presented with a red Morocco-leather-bound book surveying the history of mile running since 1868.

10　London Marathon

The inspiration of Olympic steeplechaser Chris Brasher, the first London Marathon was held on 29 March 1981, when the men's race saw Dick Beardsley (USA) and Inge Simonsen (Norway) cross the line together. The Marathon now attracts in excess of 25,000 runners, many raising money for charity.

LAST BRITISH WINNERS
of a Wimbledon title[*]

	Player	Event	Year
1	Jamie Murray	Mixed Doubles	2007
2=	Jeremy Bates	Mixed Doubles	1987
=	Jo Durie	Mixed Doubles	1987
4	John Lloyd	Mixed Doubles	1984
5	John Lloyd	Mixed Doubles	1983
6	Virginia Wade	Ladies' Singles	1977
7	Ann Jones	Ladies' Singles	1969
8	Ann Jones	Mixed Doubles	1969
9	Angela Mortimer	Ladies' Singles	1961
10	Angela Buxton	Ladies' Doubles	1956

[*] Senior title only
The last British winner of the Men's Singles (officially 'Gentlemen's Singles') was Fred Perry in 1936 and the last winners of the Men's Doubles were Pat Hughes and Raymond Tuckey, also in 1936. That year, British players won every title except the Ladies' Singles. As well as those in the last 10, the only other Britons to wins titles since the Second World War are Angela Mortimer and Anne Shilcock, who won the Ladies' Doubles in 1955.

BRITISH DRIVERS WITH THE
MOST Formula One wins[*]

	Driver	Wins
1	Nigel Mansell	31
2	Jackie Stewart	27
3	Jim Clark	25
4	Damon Hill	22
5	Stirling Moss	16
6	Graham Hill	14
7	David Coulthard	13
8	James Hunt	10
9	Lewis Hamilton	9
10=	Tony Brooks	6
=	John Surtees	6

[*] As at the end of the 2008 season

Nigel Mansell is the fourth most successful Formula One driver of all time, although his 31 wins falls well short of Michael Schumacher's all-time record total of 91. Alain Prost (51 wins) and Ayrton Senna (41) are second and third in the all-time list.

10

SPORTS AND GAMES INVENTED
in Britain

1   Baseball
Medieval manuscripts show ball games with bats, a game called 'base-ball' appears in a picture published in London in 1744 and is mentioned in Jane Austen's novel, *Northanger Abbey*, which she began writing in 1798. The game of rounders was first described in Britain 30 years later, and this or a similar game was known among British settlers in America. Abner Doubleday is sometimes credited as the game's originator in 1839, but Alexander Joy Cartwright Jr drew up baseball's first rules in 1845.

2   Cricket
Cricket evolved from medieval bat and ball games that gave rise to such variations as stool-ball and baseball. It was played in the mid-16th century and by British settlers in America as early as 1709. The first inter-county match, between Kent and London, took place 10 years later. By the mid-18th century, cricket was firmly established – especially in Kent, Sussex and Hampshire. The game's first rules were drawn up in 1744. The Marylebone Cricket Club (MCC) was established in 1787 and still governs the laws of the game.

3   Fives
A form of tennis played with a gloved hand in a court played in British public schools, most notably Rugby, Eton and Winchester. Some versions are played in a court with a buttress, reflecting the early days of the game, when it was played against chapel walls. The first pur-pose-built courts at Eton College date from 1840 and the first rules were drawn up in 1877.

4   Football
Football-like games were played in China over 2,000 years ago, and in ancient Greece and Rome, while in the Middle Ages local customs – especially on Shrove Tuesday – often centred around football matches between rival villages. Shakespeare was aware of football, referring to it in two plays. The first clubs were set up in the 1850s – Sheffield, dating from 1855, is the oldest still in existence and the Football Association (its letters 's-o-c' are the origin of the name 'soccer') founded in 1863. Inter-team games, facilitated by the growth of the railway system and work-free Saturday afternoons, led to the formation of the British Football League in the 1888–89 season, from when the first professionals also date.

5   Golf
It is arguable whether golf originated in Holland, Belgium or Scotland, but the earliest recorded reference dates from the latter in 1457, when King James II banned 'gouf', along with 'fute-ball'. His successors, however, were enthusiasts for the game – Mary, Queen of Scots was the earliest-known woman golfer. The first international game took place at Leith in 1682 when the Duke of York and a shoemaker beat two English noblemen. The Edinburgh Golfing Society was founded at Leith in 1735. The 'Royal & Ancient' St Andrews club was founded in 1754 and the Blackheath Club in England in 1766.

6 Lawn bowls

Bowls was possibly played in England as early as the 12th century, but certainly from the 13th; a tournament played in Southampton commemorates a contest dating back to 1299. Biased bowling balls were introduced in the mid-16th century, and Francis Drake's continuing with his game of bowls on Plymouth Hoe despite the sighting of the Spanish Armada on 19 July 1588 is marked as a memorable event in British history. The rules of the game were first codified in Scotland in 1849.

7 Lawn tennis

Tennis has its roots in a game played in France in an indoor court. As 'real', or royal, tennis, it was played in England from the medieval period and as 'field tennis' during the late 18th and early 19th centuries. In 1874, Major Walter Clopton Wingfield patented *Sphairistiké* (Greek for ball games), or lawn tennis, as a more vigorous version of badminton (which existed as a lawn sport developed from the ancient children's game of battledore and shuttlecock). The Marylebone Cricket Club revised Wingfield's original rules and in 1877 the game came under the aegis of the Wimbledon-based All England Croquet Club, which added the name Lawn Tennis to its own, holding the first championships in 1877.

8 Rugby

According to a dubious tradition, rugby started in 1823 at Rugby School when William Webb Ellis picked up a football and ran with it. However, various football games played in medieval Britain and Europe allowed handling of the ball, while a type of football similar to today's Australian Rules was played at Rugby almost 100 years before Webb Ellis. The first rules were drawn up in 1848, and the Rugby Football Union formed by Edwin Ash in 1871, when the laws of the game were codified. Scotland, Wales and Ireland adopted the game in the 1850s, and the first overseas clubs in the ensuing decades.

9 Stoolball

Believed to date back to the 14th century, stoolball is believed to have originated in Sussex as a game played by milkmaids, using their three-legged stools as a bat, with descriptions of such a game dating from the Elizabethan period. It resembles cricket in being played 11-a-side, but with a round bat, on a 14.6-m (16-yard) pitch with a bowling crease 10 m (16 ft) from each shoulder-height wicket, with an over consisting of eight balls. Once widely played in England, it was revived in Sussex, where it is still mainly played, especially by young women.

10 Table tennis

A version of table tennis originated as an informal after-dinner game played in houses and army messes in Victorian England. In the 1880s and 1890s, numerous commercial versions were marketed, including Gossima, introduced in 1891 by John Jacques, who in 1901 renamed and trademarked it as Ping-Pong. Celluloid balls and rubber-faced bats were introduced at the same time. At the closing of the 2008 Beijing Olympics, London Mayor Boris Johnson announced that table tennis was 'coming home' for the 2012 London Olympics, confusingly referring to 'Whiff-Whaff' – which post-dates the pioneering versions of the game.

TRADITIONAL BRITISH CHILDREN'S GAMES

1   **Blind-man's-bluff**
    This has been played in Britain since the medieval period – Samuel Pepys refers to it in his *Diary* entry for 26 December 1664, while Charles Dickens has Mr Pickwick playing it.

2   **British Bulldog**
    This widely played, tag-like game is played with many variations across the country, and has been exported to British Commonwealth countries.

3   **Conkers**
    The game played with horse chestnuts derives its name from 'conquerors' – the name given to snail shells, which were also once used in a version of it.

4   **Hide-and-seek**
    Although it existed much earlier, one of the earliest references to hide-and-seek appears in Jonathan Swift's *Gulliver's Travels* (1726).

5   **Hopscotch**
    Many versions of the game, which dates back to ancient times, have been recorded across Britain. All involve a series of jumps and hops dictated by a grid chalked on the ground.

6   **Leapfrog**
    William Shakespeare was the first to refer to leapfrog in print, in *Henry V* (1599), but versions of the game are believed to have been played in Britain since far earlier.

7   **Marbles**
    Marbles, with its extensive vocabulary to describe different types of marble and moves, has been known in Britain since before the 17th century.

8   **Postman's Knock**
    Along with variations across the country, postman's knock has been played since postmen became a familiar sight in Britain, and was well established by the late 19th century.

9   **Ring a Ring o' Roses**
    Victorian illustrator Kate Greenaway's *Mother Goose* (1881) was the first to refer to the game. Its presumed association with the Great Plague has been generally discredited.

10 **What's the Time, Mr Wolf?**
    This chasing game is believed to have evolved from the even older Fox and Chickens, which was recorded in Britain in the 16th century.

LATEST WINNERS OF THE
World Conker Championships

	Men	Women
2008	Ray Kellock	Amy Farrow
2007	Andy Hurell	Tina Stone
2006	Chris Jones	Sandy Gardner
2005	Alex Callan	Jayne Coddington
2004	Darren Foster	Alison Everett
2003	Brian Stewar	Debbie Oates
2002	Richard Swailes	Liz Gibson
2001	Neil Fraser	Celine Parachou (France)
2000	Mark Tracey	Selma Becker (Austria)
1999	Jody Tracey	Margaret Twiddy

The World Conker Championships have been held at Ashton near Oundle, Northamptonshire, since 1965. It is played to strict rules and includes individual, junior and team events. The Championships attract some 500 competitors from all over the world – all male winners have all been British, with the exception of 1998 (Helmut Kern, Germany) and 1976 (George Ramirez, Mexico) – and raise money for charity. Approximately 1,000 conkers are smashed during the course of the events.

TOP 10
BRITISH TOYS OF THE DECADES

1970s	Toy of the Year	1980s	Toy of the Year
1970	Sindy	1980	Rubik's Cube
1971	Katie Kopykat writing doll	1981	Rubik's Cube
1972	Plasticraft modelling kits	1982	Star Wars toys
1973	Mastermind board game	1983	Star Wars toys
1974	Lego Family set	1984	Masters of the Universe
1975	Lego Basic set	1985	Transformers
1976	Peter Powell kites	1986	Transformers
1977	Playmobil Playpeople	1987	Sylvanian Families
1978	Britains Combine Harvester	1988	Sylvanian Families
1979	Legoland Space kits	1989	Sylvanian Families

1990s	Toy of the Year	2000s	Toy of the Year
1990	Teenage Mutant Turtles	2000	Teksta
1991	Nintendo	2001	Bionicles
1992	WWF Wrestlers	2002	Beyblades
1993	Thunderbirds Tracey Island	2003	Beyblades
1994	Power Rangers	2004	Robosapien
1995	POGS	2005	Tamagotchi Connexion
1996	Barbie	2006	Doctor Who Cyberman Mask
1997	Teletubbies	2007	In The Night Garden Blanket Time Iggle Piggle
1998	Furby	2008	–
1999	Furby Babies	2009	–

The British Toy Retailers Association represents about 75 per cent of Britain's toy retailers. Its Toy of the Year Award, which recognizes the bestselling or highest-profile toy of the previous year, was started in 1965, when it was awarded to the James Bond Aston Martin DB5 die-cast car, released to coincide with the film *Goldfinger*. Made by Corgi, the model featured a retractable bulletproof shield, ejector seat and machine guns. It was followed by Action Man (1966), Spirograph (1967), Sindy (1968) and Hot Wheels cars (1969). At the end of the 20th century, the association awarded Lego the title of Toy of the Century, after votes had been cast by a group of retailers, together with the public, who voted over the Internet.

FAMOUS BRITISH TOYS

1   Jigsaw puzzle
    Jigsaws were made by mapmaker John Spilsbury of Drury Lane, London, in the early 1760s. His first wooden puzzles were maps designed to teach geography.

2   Meccano
    Frank Hornby of Liverpool patented 'Mechanics Made Easy' construction kits in 1901; they were renamed Meccano in 1907.

3   Dinky Toys
    Die-cast model vehicles to 1:43 scale were first made by Meccano under the name Dinky Toys in 1934.

4   Hornby-Dublo trains
    Having previously made clockwork and electric 0-gauge train sets, Hornby launched its successful Dublo (00 or 'double-0') trains in 1938.

5   Airfix Models
    The company started in 1939, making its first injection moulded plastic kit (a tractor) in 1949 and the first of its enormously popular 1:72 scale aircraft (a Spitfire) in 1955.

6   Matchbox Toys
    Toy company Lesney (taking its name from founders Leslie and Rodney Smith) launched its Matchbox range of miniature die-cast cars in 1953.

7   Scalextric
    Scalextric electric slot car racing was invented by Bertram (Fred) Francis in 1957.

8   Spirograph
    The popular drawing toy was invented in 1965 by Denys Fisher (1918–2002). It was British Toy of the Year in 1967.

9   Action Man
    The British equivalent of the US figure G.I. Joe, Action Man was launched in the UK in 1966, becoming that year's Toy of the Year.

10 Sindy dolls
    Barbie's UK rival Sindy was launched by Pedigree Dolls & Toys of Exeter in 1963, becoming Toy of the Year in both 1968 and 1970.

QUINTESSENTIALLY
BRITISH

TRADITIONAL BRITISH CUSTOMS

1 **Haxey Hood**
Held at Haxey, Humberside (formerly Lincolnshire), on Twelfth Night (6 January, unless this falls on a Sunday, when it takes place the previous day), the participants in the ancient event are a Fool with a painted face and multicoloured rag costume, a Lord and a Chief Boggin in red coats and top hats decorated with flowers and 10 further Boggins in red jumpers, accompanying numerous players who compete for 12 sackcloth hoods, but primarily for a leather hood, the goals being two public houses.

2 **Twelfth Night**
A number of traditional Twelfth Night (6 January) customs in Britain involved serving cakes and wine. One that survives is Baddeley Cake ceremony at the Theatre Royal, Drury Lane, London, funded by a bequest from actor Robert Baddeley (1732–94), a former cook.

3 **Up Helly-Aa**
The most celebrated fire festival in Europe, the Up Helly-Aa takes place in Lerwick, Shetland, at the end of January. Traditionally, blazing tar barrels were drawn through the streets, but since 1889 a replica Viking longship is dragged along by a torchlit procession with participants dressed as characters from Norse legends, following which songs are sung and the ship is set alight.

4 **Nutters Dance**
The Britannia Coco-Nut Dancers, or 'Nutters' of Bacup, Lancashire, traditionally perform on Easter Saturday. They wear white hats, black tops with sashes, striped kilts and wooden clogs and have blackened faces. They use wooden discs on their hands and knees to beat a rhythm. The custom is of unknown origin, but great antiquity.

5 **Hare Pie Scramble and Bottle Kicking**
Held at Hallaton, Leicestershire, on Easter Monday, the custom was first recorded in the early 18th century, but is much older. It involves a scramble for a hare pie between the villagers of Hallaton and neighbouring Medbourne, followed by a free-for-all football match played by large teams across a stream, with 'bottles' – actually three small barrels, two of which contain beer – as the 'balls'.

6 **Helston Furry Dance**
On or about 8 May, Helston, Cornwall, celebrates the arrival of spring with the Furry or Flora dance, a series of dances for different age groups, the principal one at midday performed by men in morning suits and top hats and women in floral dresses and summer hats. A relatively modern mystery play has also been incorporated into the proceedings. The 'Floral Dance' song was composed by Kate Moss (1881–1947) in 1911, a brass band version of it charting at UK No.2 in 1977.

7   Cheese Rolling

Taking place on Spring Bank Holiday Monday at Cooper's Hill, Brockworth, Gloucestershire, the custom, which dates from the early 19th century or earlier, involves rolling a Double Gloucester cheese down the steep hill with contestants hurtling after it. Injuries are often sustained in the three men's races and one women's race, the first competitor to cross the line winning the cheese.

8   Dunmow Flitch Trials

Claimed to date back to 1104, so already an ancient custom when it was mentioned in Chaucer's *Canterbury Tales*, the Flitch Trials take place in July every four years (last in 2008, next in 2012) in Great Dunmow, Essex. Couples who have been married for at least a year appear before a judge and jury of six maidens and six bachelors. If they are able to prove that they are happily married, they can claim a flitch, or side of bacon, and are carried shoulder-high to the town's marketplace. One of the four winning couples in 2008 was from the USA.

9   Abbots Bromley Horn Dance

The custom takes place at Abbots Bromley, Staffordshire, on Wakes Monday, the day after the first Sunday after 4 September. The horns that give it its name – ancient reindeer antlers providing a clue as its antiquity – are housed in the church. Twelve male dancers wear medieval costume, accompanied by a man dressed as Maid Marian, a hobby horse, a Fool and a child with a bow and arrow and another with a triangle.

10   Lewes Bonfire

In Lewes, East Sussex, Guy Fawkes Night (5 November) has been merged with a commemoration of the burning of 17 Protestant martyrs in the town during the reign of Mary I. Six bonfire societies (Borough, Cliffe, Commercial Square, Southover, South Street and Waterloo), plus others from outlying towns and villages, parade through Lewes in fancy dress with blazing torches, lay wreaths and say prayers before going to their respective bonfire sites for spectacular firework displays at which 'clergy' are pelted with fireworks and effigies of Pope Paul V and 'enemies of bonfire' are exploded.

10
TRADITIONAL BRITISH NURSERY RHYMES

1 'Three Blind Mice'
   The earliest-known printed version of the rhyme appears as one of his 'pleasant roundelaies' in *Deuteromelia, or The Seconde Part of Musiks Melodie* (1609) by Thomas Ravenscroft, a former chorister at St Paul's Cathedral.

2 'Old King Cole'
   The rhyme first appeared in *Useful Transactions in Philosophy* (1709) by William King (1663–1712).

3 'London Bridge is Falling Down'
   The earliest printed version is in *Namby Pamby* (1725) by Henry Carey (*c*.1687–1743).

4 'Oranges and Lemons'
   The rhyme, which lists various London churches and the sounds of their bells, was first printed in the anonymous *Tom Thumb's Pretty Song Book* (1744), the earliest book to print 'Sing a Song of Sixpence', 'Who Killed Cock Robin?' and other well-known verses.

5 'This is the House that Jack Built'
   The nursery rhyme first appeared in about 1755 in pioneer children's book publisher John Newbery's *Nurse Truelove's New-Year's-Gift, or the Book of Books for Children*.

6 'This Little Piggy Went to Market'
   Although the title line appears in various collections, the full version of the rhyme appeared in about 1760 in *The Famous Tommy Thumb's Little Story-Book*.

7 'Jack and Jill'
   The popular rhyme was first printed in John Newbery's *Mother Goose's Melody, or Sonnets for the Cradle* (*c*.1765).

8 'Old Mother Hubbard'
   Its first appearance was in *Nancy Cock's Pretty Song Book for all Little Misses and Masters* (1780), but it has been claimed that it refers to the much earlier Catherine of Aragon.

9 'There was an Old Woman Who Lived in a Shoe'
   A number of women have been identified with the old woman of the rhyme, which first appeared in *Gammer Gurton's Garland, or the Nursery Parnassus* (1784) by Joseph Ritson.

10 'Pussy Cat Pussy Cat'
   The rhyme first appeared in print in 1805 in *Songs for the Nursery* by Benjamin Tabart (1767–1833), who also introduced the verse 'One Two, Buckle My Shoe'.

PATRIOTIC BRITISH SONGS

1 'The British Grenadiers'
One of the oldest British marching songs, dating from the early 17th century, its author is unknown. It is traditionally played at Trooping the Colour.

2 'God Save the Queen' (or King)
The author of the British national anthem is unknown, and probably predates the earliest-known printed version of 1744. On 3 June 2002, during the Queen's Golden Jubilee, it was famously played on guitar by Brian May on the roof of Buckingham Palace.

3 'Rule, Britannia!'
With lyrics by James Thomson and music by Thomas Arne, 'Rule, Britannia!' was first performed in a masque for Frederick, Prince of Wales, on 1 August 1740.

4 'Heart of Oak'
The lyrics are by the British actor David Garrick, with music by William Boyce. It was first performed in the pantomime *Harlequin's Invasion* at Drury Lane, London, in 1759.

5 'Land of Hope and Glory'
Written as a Coronation Ode for Edward VII, with lyrics by A(rthur) C(hristopher) Benson and music by Edward Elgar, it was first performed in 1902.

6 'I Vow to Thee, My Country'
A poem originally written by Cecil Spring-Rice in 1908 and later revised, it was set to music in 1921 by Gustav Holst by adapting 'Jupiter' from his *The Planets*.

7 'It's a Long Way to Tipperary'
A 1912 music-hall song with words and music by Jack Judge and Harry Williams, it became a popular marching song during the First World War.

8 'Keep the Home Fires Burning'
Written in 1915 by Lena Guilbert Ford with music by Ivor Novello, the song was one of the most popular of the First World War.

9 'Pack Up Your Troubles'
Written by 'George Asaf' (George Henry Powell) with music by his brother Felix Powell in 1915, it became a well-known First World War marching song.

10 'The White Cliffs of Dover'
Composed in 1941 by two Americans, Walter Kent (music) and Nat Burton (lyrics), Vera Lynn's version became an anthem of the Second World War.

THE 10

FIRST GILBERT AND SULLIVAN OPERAS

	Opera	Theatre*	Initial run performances	Opening
1	*Thespis*	Gaiety Theatre	63	26 Dec 1871
2	*Trial by Jury*	Royalty Theatre	131	25 Mar 1875
3	*The Sorcerer*	Opera Comique	178	17 Nov 1877
4	*H.M.S. Pinafore*	Opera Comique	571	25 May 1878
5	*The Pirates of Penzance*	Opera Comique†	363	3 Apr 1880
6	*Patience*	Opera Comique†	578	23 Apr 1881
7	*Iolanthe*	Savoy Theatre	398	25 Nov 1882
8	*Princess Ida*	Savoy Theatre	246	5 Jan 1884
9	*The Mikado*	Savoy Theatre	672	14 Mar 1885
10	*Ruddigore*	Savoy Theatre	288	22 Jan 1887

* All London
† Premiere in New York, 31 December 1879
The partnership of librettist W. S. (William Schwenck) Gilbert (1836–1911) and composer Arthur Seymour Sullivan (1842–1900) spanned 25 years, during which they created 14 comic operas, many of which are still frequently performed. Their first 10 were followed by *The Yeomen of the Guard* (1888), *The Gondoliers* (1889), *Utopia, Limited* (1893) and *The Grand Duke* (1896). Sullivan was knighted in 1883 and Gilbert in 1905.

TOP 10
FAVOURITE HYMNS
in Britain

1   'How Great Thou Art'
Music from a Swedish folk tune, words from a Russian hymn translated by Stuart Wesley Keene Hine (1899–1989).

2   'Dear Lord and Father of Mankind'
Music by Charles Hubert Parry (1848–1918), based on a poem by John Greenleaf Whittier (1807–92).

3   'The Day Thou Gavest'
Music by Clement Cotterill Scholefield (1839–1904), words by John Ellerton (1826–93).

4   'Be Thou My Vision'
Irish traditional melody, words translated by Mary Byrne (1880–1931) and Eleanor Hull (1860–1935).

5   'Love Divine, All Loves Excelling'
Music by William Penfro Rowlands (1860–1937), words by Charles Wesley (1707–88).

6   'Be Still, for the Presence of The Lord'
Music and words by David J. Evans (b. 1957)

7   'Make Me a Channel'
Music by Sebastian Temple (b. 1928), arranged by James Whitbourn (b. 1963), words from a prayer attributed to St Francis of Assisi (c.1182–1226).

8   'Guide Me, O Thou Great Redeemer'
Music by John Hughes (1873–1932), words by William Williams (1717–91) and Peter Williams (1727–96).

9   'In Christ Alone'
Music by Keith Getty (b. 1974), words by Stuart Townend (b. 1963).

10 'Shine, Jesus, Shine'
Music and words by Graham Kendrick (b. 1950), arranged by James Whitbourn (b. 1963).

Based on a poll conducted by BBC *Songs of Praise*.

BRITISH HAUNTED HOUSES

1 ## 50 Berkeley Square, London
The Georgian house, on the west side of Berkeley Square, since 1939 the premises of anti-quarian booksellers Maggs Bros, was described in *The Times* of 29 April 1873 as 'the haunted house', and is even claimed as 'the most haunted house in London'. Its spectral inhabitants are said to include the ghost of the lunatic brother of a tenant called Du Pre who had been imprisoned in the attic, a child that died there and a young woman who committed suicide. One person, named in some accounts as 'Sir Robert Warboys', died of fright after spending a night there, as did a man who fell through a window in terror and was impaled on spiked railings. Its horrific reputation inspired Edward Bulwer Lytton to write his story *The Haunted and the Haunters* (1859).

2 ## Blickling Hall, Norfolk
Now a National Trust property, the Jacobean house was built on the site of the home of the Boleyn family, and in about 1500 was the birthplace of Henry VIII's second wife Anne. It is said that every year on 19 May, the anniversary of her execution at the Tower of London, her ghost arrives in a ghostly carriage, with her decapitated head in her lap – an added frisson is that the driver of her carriage is also headless.

3 ## Borley Rectory, Essex
The original house, which was seriously damaged by fire in 1939, was built on the site of a convent. In 1863, sightings of ghosts of nuns and other phenomena prompted investiga-tion by the Society for Psychical Research and ghost-hunter Harry Price, which allegedly uncovered 'evidence' of a malicious poltergeist. Subsequent manifestations were widely reported in the press, the house gaining the media reputation as the 'most haunted in England'.

4 ## Glamis Castle, Angus
The ancestral home of the Bowes-Lyon family, the birthplace of Princess Margaret, is considered Scotland's most haunted castle. As well as a legendary monster, it boasts a large gallery of ghosts that includes Macbeth; a Grey Lady (identified as Lady Janet Douglas, burned at the stake in Edinburgh on 17 July 1537 for attempting to poison James V); a woman with no tongue; 'Earl Beardie' (Alexander, Earl Crawford), who is said to be eternally dicing with the devil; and a 'mad earl' who patrols the castle ramparts.

5 ## Hampton Court, Surrey
The ghost of Jane Seymour, who died at Hampton Court shortly after giving birth to Edward VI, is one of many that haunt this house. Others include Catherine Howard, an apparition of whom re-enacts her flight from Henry VIII's guards; Henry VIII himself; Anne Boleyn; Cardinal Wolsey; Sybil Penn, who nursed Princess Elizabeth I through small-pox but succumbed herself in 1562 (she was buried there but her tomb was disturbed in

1829); and various unidentified cavaliers. As recently as 2003, closed-circuit security cameras were reported to have picked up ghostly images.

6 Markyate Cell, Hertfordshire

The life and career of Lady Katherine Ferrers, *née* Fanshaw, have become so intertwined with legend that it is impossible to disentangle them. It is popularly believed that in the mid-17th century she operated as a highwaywoman, nicknamed the 'Wicked Lady', and that in 1660, after being wounded during a robbery, bled to death at her home, Markyate Cell – where she is said to have hidden her loot, which has never been found. In 1894 writer Augustus Hare noted her apparition at the house but it has also been seen on horseback patrolling nearby roads.

7 Michaelham Priory, East Sussex

Founded in 1229, the moated Augustinian priory is reputed to be haunted by several ghosts, including a 'Grey Lady' in the gatehouse, a woman in Elizabethan costume in the Tudor wing of the house and a mysterious black-clad phantom that floats diagonally from a corner of the ceiling to the floor as it descends the line of a staircase that no longer exists.

8 Raynham Hall, Norfolk

The 'Brown Lady' of Raynham Hall is the subject of an alleged ghost photograph, showing her on the staircase and reproduced in *Country Life* on 26 December 1936. She is claimed to be Dolly Townshend, the sister of Robert Walpole and wife of politician Charles Townshend, who died of smallpox in 1726, but was rumoured to have been walled up in the house. She was seen by members of the Townshend family and visitors to the house, including the author Captain Frederick Marryat.

9 Theatre Royal, London

One of Britain's most haunted theatres, the cast of ghosts at the Theatre Royal, Drury Lane, include the 'Man in Grey', an 18th-century dandy stabbed to death in the theatre whose skeleton was found walled up there. He is said to be benign, his appearance at matinees considered a good omen for the production. Other ghosts include Charles II and his attendants; Charles Macklin, who in 1735 killed fellow actor Thomas Hallam by poking him in the eye with a stick – although why the killer rather than his victim haunts the theatre has not been explained; the clown Joseph Grimaldi and comedian Dan Leno.

10 Tower of London

The Tower of London's bloody reputation has led to its being described as the most haunted place in Britain. Its ghosts include those of the Princes in the Tower (Edward V and Richard Duke of York); Anne Boleyn with her retinue, usually sighted in St Peter ad Vincula; Catherine Howard; Lady Jane Grey and her husband Guildford Dudley; Sir Walter Raleigh; the Countess of Salisbury, whose bungled execution is re-enacted by her ghost; a spectral funeral carriage and even a phantom bear from the Tower Menagerie.

10

LEGENDARY BRITISH CREATURES

1 Afanc
A Welsh lake monster whose appearance has been variously described: sometimes it is likened to a huge, hairy man riding a giant horse, but at others to a crocodile or a beaver.

2 Barghest
A fierce, ghostly black dog said to live in the north of England. A similar creature, the Black Shuck, lives on the coast of Norfolk, Essex and Suffolk.

3 Beast of Bodmin
Along with such creatures as the Beast of Exmoor, this is one of many giant wild cats claimed to have been sighted across Britain.

4 Boobrie
This gigantic duck is said to dwell in the Highlands of Scotland. It roars like an angry bull and eats cattle and sheep.

5 Enfield Beast
This British heraldic creature appears on the coat of arms of the London Borough of Enfield. It is the ultimate hybrid, with the head of a fox, the chest of a greyhound, the body of a lion, the hind legs and tail of a wolf and the talons of an eagle.

6 Lambton Worm
This dragon-like monster was said to terrorize the people of Durham, until it was slain by Sir John Lambton. It appears in Bram Stoker's *The Lair of the White Worm*.

7 Loch Ness Monster
One of the most widely known British mythological animals, 'Nessie' is said to have dwelt in Loch Ness for over 1,000 years. It has been the subject of many hunts and hoaxes.

8 Nuckelavee
The terrifying and malevolent centaur-like nuckelavee appears in the folklore of the Orkneys. The only way to escape its clutches is to cross running water.

9 Selkie
In Celtic mythology, the selkie is a seal that can transform itself into a human, sometimes marrying into human families, usually with tragic results.

10 Water Leaper
The Water Leaper, known in Wales as Llamhigyn Y Dwr, is said to resemble a giant frog or toad, with the wings of a bat and a reptilian tail that skims across the water.

UNUSUAL BRITISH NAMES

1 ## Minty Badger
Badger is found as a surname in Warwickshire. Minty was recorded as marrying in Southam in 1866, while Smiley Badger was born in Napton in about 1888.

2 ## Nicholas If-Jesus-Christ-Had-Not-Died-For-Thee-Thou-Hadst-Been-Damned Barebon
Following the Great Fire of London in 1666, Barebon (c.1640–98), the son of Praise-God Barbon [sic]. invented fire insurance.

3 ## Philadelphia Bunnyface
Her surname, in a 1722 Cornish will, may be a corruption of 'Boniface'.

4 ## Grimwood Death
Born c.1810 and died in Hartismere, Suffolk, in 1884, he was one of several generations of Grimwood Deaths, the most recent (spelling his surname De'Ath) dying in 2002.

5 ## One Too Many Gouldstone
Born in West Ham, Essex, in 1870, he was given this name by parents dismayed at his arrival – like those of Not Wanted James Colvill and Lewis Unexpected Smith.

6 ## Neglected Heaks
Baptized in Aylesbury, Buckinghamshire, 3 February 1627, she was so-called 'because she had no God father or God mother prepared at the time of Baptizing'.

7 ## Offspring Jeeves
'Offspring' sometimes appears in birth records when a newborn baby has yet to be named, but in the 19th century was used as a first name by several families in Arlesey, Bedfordshire.

8 ## Bamlet Neptune Switzer
Bamlet Neptune Switzer (1863–1927), curate of Crowborough, Sussex, was born at sea, hence his middle name.

9 ## Fare-well Sykes
Honley Yorkshire-born Fare-well, who was drowned in 1865, was the brother of Live-well, Do-well and Die-well Sykes.

10 ## Benjamin Teapot
Born in Neath, Glamorgan, 1858, his name started a brief local trend: another Benjamin Teapot was born in Neath in 1867, followed by one in 1878.

BRITISH END OF THE WORLD PROPHETS

1   **Richard Harvey** (*c*.1560–1630)
    In 1583 Saffron Walden-born astrologer Harvey prophesied that when the conjunction of
    Saturn and Jupiter occurred at noon on Sunday, 28 April 1583, a great wind would spring
    up, heralding the end of the world. When it failed to happen, he was widely mocked and
    satirized in London's theatres and in songs that ridiculed his predictions.

2   **Lady Eleanor Davies** (1590–1652)
    As a result of a vision on 25 July 1625 in which a heavenly voice told her the world
    would end in 19 years, she was convinced the event would occur in 1644. Her bizarre acts,
    including occupying the bishop's throne in Lichfield cathedral and declaring herself
    primate and her outspoken prophecies and numerous pamphlets led to her being commit-
    ted to Bedlam as a lunatic and then imprisoned in the Tower of London from 1638 to 1640.

3   **Solomon Eccles** (*c*.1617–82)
    In 1665 Eccles, a Quaker, wandered around London naked with a pan of blazing
    sulphur on his head, crying, 'Repent! Repent!' and warned worshippers at St Mary's
    Aldermanbury of the end of the world. He was arrested but on his release travelled to
    Barbados and America, where he again prophesied doom and was again jailed.

4   **John Napier** (1550–1617)
    The Scottish astrologer and mathematician, inventor of weapons and logarithms and
    popularizer of the decimal point, predicted that the world would end between 1688 and
    1700 – by which time he was long dead.

5   **William Whiston** (1667–1752)
    An eminent theologian, prolific writer on subjects from geology to demonology and
    mathematician who was convinced that the Biblical Flood had been caused by a comet,
    Whiston predicted that another would hit and destroy Earth on 16 October 1736. Many
    took to boats, fearing the coming deluge, which failed to happen.

6   **Richard Brothers** (1757–1824)
    Brothers, a former sailor, attracted followers after apparently predicting the assassination
    of Gustavus III of Sweden and the guillotining of Louis XVI. When, in 1795, he prophesied
    imminent catastrophe and that George III would abdicate in his favour, he was declared
    insane and imprisoned, but continued to claim that an earthquake was about to destroy
    London. One of his last pronouncements in his *A Correct Account of the Invasion and
    Conquest of this Island by the Saxons* (1822), was to proclaim that the British were one of the
    lost tribes of Israel.

7 Mother Shipton (16th century)

A witch and prophetess supposedly living in York during the reign of Henry VIII, Mother Shipton was claimed to have predicted the Spanish Armada, Civil War and Great Fire of London. In 1856, Charles Dickens published a story about Mother Shipton in his magazine *Household Words*, prompting renewed interest in her prognostications. A set of rhymes purporting to be by her and published in 1862 included the couplet:

The world then to an end shall come
In Eighteen Hundred and Eighty One.

Before the predicted date, in 1873, their publisher, a Brighton bookseller, Charles Hindley, admitted he had made them up.

8 John Cumming (1807–81)

Cumming, a Scottish Presbyterian minister and beekeeper, made a study of the biblical books of Genesis and Daniel, from which he concluded that the world would end in 1867, publishing his predictions in pamphlets with titles such as *The Great Tribulation, or Things Coming on the Earth* (1859). When it failed to do so, and he was discovered to be negotiating a 21-year extension on the lease on his house, his reputation as a prophet was destroyed.

9 Charles Piazzi Smyth (1819–1900)

From his research on the dimensions of the Great Pyramid of Giza, Egypt, the Astronomer Royal for Scotland concluded that the world would end between 1892 and 1911. By the time this failed to happen, Smyth was dead and buried in a pyramid-shaped tomb in Sharrow, near Ripon, Yorkshire.

10 Sir Isaac Newton (1643–1727)

Newton's book *Observations upon the Prophecies of Daniel and the Apocalypse of St John*, published in 1733, six years after his death, indicates his belief that the end of the world would occur in 2000.

FIRST *CARRY ON* FILMS

	Film	Release*
1	*Carry On Sergeant*	Aug 1958
2	*Carry On Nurse*	Mar 1959
3	*Carry On Teacher*	Aug 1959
4	*Carry On Constable*	Feb 1960
5	*Carry On Regardless*	Mar 1961
6	*Carry On Cruising*	Apr 1962
7	*Carry On Cabby*	Jun 1963
8	*Carry On Jack*	Nov 1963
9	*Carry On Spying*	Jun 1964
10	*Carry On Cleo*	Nov 1964

* London release date; provincial releases generally later

This original series of hugely successful British comedy films spanned 20 years. The first 10 were followed by *Carry On Cowboy* (1965), *Carry On Screaming* (1966), *Carry On – Don't Lose Your Head* (1966), *Carry On – Follow That Camel* (1967), *Carry On Doctor* (1967), *Carry On Up the Khyber* (1968), *Carry On Again Doctor* (1969), *Carry On Camping* (1969), *Carry On Up the Jungle* (1970), *Carry On Loving* (1970), *Carry On Henry* (1971), *Carry On at Your Convenience* (1971), *Carry On Abroad* (1972), *Carry On Matron* (1972), *Carry On Girls* (1973), *Carry On Dick* (1974), *Carry On Behind* (1975), *Carry On England* (1976) and *Carry On Emmannuelle* (1978). The last of the series, *Carry On Columbus* (1992) was an attempt to revive the series, while a long-mooted *Carry On London* is scheduled for 2009.

BRITISH TV SITCOM WRITING TEAMS

1 **Ray Galton (b. UK, 1930) and Alan Simpson (b. UK, 1929)**
Together they wrote 56 episodes of *Hancock's Half Hour* (1956–61) and 57 of *Steptoe and Son* (1962–74).

2 **Ronald Wolfe (b. UK, 1924) and Ronald Chesney (b. UK, 1922)**
After creating and writing *The Rag Trade* (1961–3), the duo wrote 68 episodes of *On the Buses* (1969–73).

3 **Dick Clement (b. UK, 1937) and Ian La Frenais (b. UK, 1937)**
The two wrote *The Likely Lads* (1964–6) and *Whatever Happened to the Likely Lads?* (1973), *Porridge* (1974–7) and *Auf Wiedersehen, Pet* (1983–6).

4 **John Esmonde (UK, 1937–2008) and Bob Larbey (b. UK, 1934)**
Their prolific writing credits include *Please Sir!* (1968–72), *The Good Life* (1975–8), *Ever Decreasing Circles* (1984–9) and *Brush Strokes* (1986–91).

5 **Jimmy Perry (b. UK, 1923) and David Croft (b. UK, 1922)**
The pair created and wrote 80 episodes of *Dad's Army* (1968–77), 56 episodes of *It Ain't Half Hot Mum* (1974–81) and 58 of *Hi-de-Hi!* (1980–88).

6 **Jeremy Lloyd (b. UK, 1932) and David Croft (b. UK, 1922)**
Lloyd and Croft penned 69 episodes of *Are You Being Served?* (1972–85) and 67 of *'Allo 'Allo!* (1982–92).

7 **John Cleese (b. UK, 1939) and Connie Booth (b. USA, 1944)**
John Cleese and his then wife, Connie Booth, co-wrote and starred in all 12 episodes of *Fawlty Towers* (1975–9).

8 **Antony Jay (b. UK, 1930) and Jonathan Lynn (b. UK, 1943)**
Their principal work together was *Yes Minister* (1980–84) and its follow-up, *Yes Prime Minister* (1986–8).

9 **Richard Curtis (b. New Zealand, 1956) and Ben Elton (b. UK, 1959)**
Curtis wrote the first *Blackadder* series, *The Blackadder* (1983), with Rowan Atkinson, but was joined by Ben Elton for *Blackadder II* (1986), *Blackadder III* (1987) and *Blackadder Goes Forth* (1989).

10 **Ricky Gervais (b. UK, 1961) and Stephen Merchant (b. UK, 1974)**
Their award-winning series to date have been *The Office* (2001–3) and *Extras* (2005–7).

CLASSIC *MONTY PYTHON* SKETCHES

	Sketch	Episode	First broadcast
1	The Funniest Joke in the World	Episode 1: 'Whither Canada'	5 Oct 1969
2	Nudge Nudge	Episode 3: 'How to Recognize Different Types of Trees from Quite a Long Way Away'	19 Oct 1969
3	Crunchy Frog	Episode 6: 'It's the Arts'	23 Nov 1969
4	Dead Parrot	Episode 8: 'Full Frontal Nudity'	7 Dec 1969
5	Upper Class Twit of the Year	Episode 12: 'The Naked Ant'	4 Jan 1970
6	Ministry of Silly Walks	Episode 14: 'Face the Press'	15 Sep 1970
7	The Spanish Inquisition	Episode 15: 'The Spanish Inquisition'	22 Sep 1970
8	Spam	Episode 25: 'Spam'	15 Dec 1970
9	The Argument Clinic	Episode 29: 'The Money Programme'	2 Nov 1972
10	Cheese Shop	Episode 33: 'Salad Days'	30 Nov 1972

BRITISH DESIGN ICONS

	Icon	Designer	Date
1	Concorde	British Aircraft Corporation/Aérospatiale	1969
2	London Underground map	Harry Beck	1931
3	Supermarine Spitfire	R. J. Mitchell	1936
4	Mini	Alec Issigonis	1959
5	World Wide Web	Tim Berners-Lee	1991
6	Routemaster bus	Douglas Scott, A. A. Durant and Colin Curtis	1954
7	Catseye	Percy Shaw	1934
8	*Tomb Raider* video game	Cors Design	1996
9	*Grand Theft Auto* video game	DMA Design	1997
10	K2 Red telephone box	Giles Gilbert Scott	1926

As voted on in a 2006 poll conducted by the Design Museum, London, and BBC2's *Culture Show*, in which 211,700 votes were cast.

10 EVENTS IN THE ENGLISH SEASON

	Event	Date*	First held
1	Royal Ascot	16–20 Jun	1711
2	Royal Academy Summer Exhibition	1 Jun–31 Aug	1769
3	Goodwood races	28 Jul–1 Aug	1812
4	Cowes Week	1–8 Aug	1826
5	Henley Royal Regatta	1–5 Jul	1839
6	Chelsea Flower Show	19–23 May	1862
7	Wimbledon	22 Jun–5 Jul	1877
8	Crufts	5–8 Mar	1886
9	Last Night of the Proms	12 Sep	1895
10	Glyndebourne opera	21 May–30 Aug	1934

* Dates are variable – provisional for 2009

Traditionally, the Season was a series of events held in London during the summer months and attended by members of the English upper class. During the Season, debutantes attended a number of balls, culminating in Queen Charlotte's Ball, which dates from 1780, and were presented at court, a practice that continued until 1958. Although many of the formal elements of the social season died out after the First World War, a number of events persist, some of them staged in aid of charity and latterly with corporate sponsorship and hospitality to the fore, as exemplified in such innovations as Cartier International Polo.

TOP 10

FLOWERS GROWN
in the UK

	Seeds	Bulbs
1	Sweet pea	Narcissus
2	Night-scented stock	Tulip
3	Lobelia	Crocus
4	Nasturtium	Hyacinth
5	French marigold	Dahlia
6	Alyssum	Gladioli
7	Godetia	Begonia
8	Impatiens (Busy Lizzie)	Snowdrop
9	Sunflower	Anemone
10	Geranium	Scilla

Source: Suttons Seeds

TOP 10

LONGEST-SERVING *BLUE PETER* PRESENTERS

	Name/dates	Duration Years	Months	Days
1	John Noakes (30 Dec 1965–26 Jun 1978)	12	5	27
2	Peter Purves (16 Nov 1967–23 Mar 1978)	10	4	7
3	Konnie Huq (1 Dec 1997–23 Jan 2008)	10	1	21
4	Valerie Singleton (3 Sep 1962–3 Jul 1972)	9	10	0*
5	Christopher Trace (16 Oct 1958–24 Jul 1967)	8	9	8
6	Simon Groom (15 May 1978–23 Jun 1986)	8	1	8
7	Matt Baker (25 Jun 1999–26 Jun 2006)	7	0	1
8	Lesley Judd (5 May 1972–12 Apr 1979)	6	10	28
9	Simon Thomas (8 Jan 1999–25 Apr 2005)	6	3	17
10	Diane-Louise Jordan (25 Jan 1990–26 Feb 1996)	6	1	1

* Plus occasional subsequent appearances

TRADITIONAL PANTOMIMES' FIRST PERFORMANCES in the UK

	Pantomime	Year
1	*Robinson Crusoe*	1781
2	*Aladdin*	1788
3	*Little Red Riding Hood*	1803
4	*Cinderella*	1804
5	*Mother Goose*	1805
6	*Sleeping Beauty*	1806
7	*Dick Whittington*	1814
8	*Sinbad the Sailor*	1814
9	*Puss in Boots*	1818
10	*Jack and the Beanstalk*	1819

Shows such as *Harlequin Sorcerer* (1716), *The Loves of Mars and Venus* (1717) and *Jack the Giant Killer* (1773) were all described as 'pantomimes', but *Robinson Crusoe*, written by Irish playwright Richard Brinsley Sheridan and first performed at the Theatre Royal, Drury Lane, London on 29 January 1781, was the first we would recognize as such. Such elements as the pantomime dame and the principal boy being played by a woman gradually emerged as the genre developed during the 19th century, establishing a canon of works that are still performed across Britain every Christmas.

FIRST WOMEN'S INSTITUTES
in the UK

	Location	Founded
1	Llanfairpwll, Anglesey	17 Sep 1915
2	Cefn, Denbigh	13 Oct 1915
3	Trefant, Denbigh	14 Oct 1915
4	Wallisdown, Dorset	19 Nov 1915
5	Singleton, West Sussex	1 Dec 1915
6	Hamworthy, Dorset	Dec 1915*
7	Criccieth, Caernafon	17 Jan 1916
8	Holyhead, Anglesey	25 Jan 1916
9	Kemsing, Kent	26 Jan 1916
10	Upton, Dorset	1 Feb 1916

* Precise date unknown

Britain's first Women's Institutes were established as a response to the First World War, to encourage Britons to be self-sufficient in growing and preparing their own food. Madge Watt, a recent arrival from Canada, where such an organization had existed since 1897, set up the first in the Anglesey village the extremely long name of which is generally abbreviated to Llanfairpwll. By 2008 there were some 6,700 WIs in England and Wales with a total membership of 205,000. The equivalent organization in Scotland is the Scottish Women's Rural Institutes, which dates from 1917.

LIVING AND
DYING IN
BRITAIN

PLACES WITH THE MOST BIRTHS
in England and Wales

	Location*	Birthrate†
1	Barking & Dagenham	2.52
2	Newham	2.49
3	Rutland	2.48
4	Blackburn and Darwen	2.44
5	Slough	2.38
6=	Boston	2.37
=	Luton	2.37
8	Oldham	2.36
9	Bradford	2.33
10	Peterborough	2.31

* Based on local authority area
† Total fertility rate (average number of children born to each woman), 2006
Source: National Statistics, *Population Trends No.133* (Autumn 2008)

THE 10
PLACES WITH THE FEWEST
BIRTHS in England and Wales

	Location*	Birthrate†
1	Westminster	1.21
2	Camden	1.27
3	Exeter	1.28
4	Durham	1.33
5	Kensington & Chelsea	1.37
6=	Cambridge	1.39
=	Ceredigion	1.39
=	Runnymede	1.39
9	Lancaster	1.40
10	Oxford	1.42

* Based on local authority area
† Total fertility rate (average number of children born to each woman), 2006
Source: National Statistics, *Population Trends No.133* (Autumn 2008)

PLACES WHERE LIFESPANS ARE LONGEST in the UK[*]

	Location	Women	Average age of death Men	All
1	Eastbourne West, East Sussex	82.7	77.5	80.6
2=	Bexhill, East Sussex	82.5	77.8	80.5
=	Worthing Central, West Sussex	82.8	76.8	80.5
4	Hove Coast, East Sussex	82.7	75.5	80.0
5	Poole Branksome, Dorset	82.3	76.5	79.9
6	Bournemouth Boscombe, Dorset	82.2	75.7	79.5
7=	Bournemouth Central, Dorset	82.4	75.2	79.4
=	East Devon Rural, Devon	81.6	77.0	79.4
=	Worthing Rustington, West Sussex	81.1	77.3	79.4
10=	Harrogate, North Yorkshire	81.9	74.6	79.1
=	New Milton, Hampshire	81.3	76.5	79.1

* Based on a survey of mortality rates in 1,283 places in the UK
Source: Mary Shaw, *et al, The Grim Reaper's Road Map: An Atlas of Mortality in Britain* (The Policy Press, 2008)

PLACES WHERE LIFESPANS ARE SHORTEST in the UK*

	Location	Average age of death		
		Women	Men	All
1	Glasgow Easterhouse, West Central Scotland	69.6	63.3	66.4
2	Livingston Central, East Central Scotland	70.8	63.7	67.2
3	Cumbernauld, Lanarkshire	70.9	63.9	67.3
4	Sparkbrook, West Midlands	71.2	65.7	68.1
5	Harlesden, London	72.7	65.4	68.6
6=	Linwood, West Central Scotland	72.5	65.0	68.7
=	Johnstone, West Central Scotland	72.0	65.7	68.7
8	Glasgow Castlemilk, West Central Scotland	71.8	65.9	68.8
9	Tamworth Urban, Staffordshire	71.9	66.7	69.0
10	Moss Side, Greater Manchester	73.6	65.2	69.1

* Based on a survey of mortality rates in 1,283 places in the UK
Source: Mary Shaw, *et al, The Grim Reaper's Road Map: An Atlas of Mortality in Britain* (The Policy Press, 2008)

MOST COMMON REASONS FOR VISITS TO THE DOCTOR in the UK

	Complaint	Rate*
1	Hypertensive diseases	946
2	Dermatitis and eczema	897
3	Skin disorders	884
4	Acute upper respiratory infections	802
5	Disorders of the eye	792
6	Disorders of the ear and mastoid process	731
7	Other acute lower respiratory infections	716
8	Chronic lower respiratory diseases	696
9	Dorsopathies (back problems)	640
10	Non-inflammatory female disorders	543

* Patients consulting per 10,000
Source: Office of Health Economics, *Compendium of Health Statistics*, 17th edition, 2005–6

COUNTRIES OF RESIDENCE FOR PEOPLE MARRYING at Gretna Green

	Country of residence	Bride	Groom	Total (2007)
1	England	2,483	2,493	4,976
2	Scotland	492	495	987
3	Wales	159	161	320
4	Northern Ireland	74	74	148
5	Ireland	57	59	116
6	Germany	20	17	37
7	Australia	15	13	28
8=	Spain	12	11	23
=	USA	14	9	23
10	France	11	10	21

Source: General Register Office for Scotland
In 2007 there were 4,452 marriages registered at Gretna (a fall on the record year of 2005, when there were 5,555), with these representing the principal countries of origin.

TOP 10

OLDEST SCHOOLS
in the UK

	School	Founded
1	The King's School, Canterbury	597
2	The King's School, Rochester	604
3	St Peter's School, York	627
4	Beverley Grammar School	700
5	Warwick School	914
6	St Alban's School	948
7	The King's School, Ely	970
8	Salisbury Cathedral School	1091
9	Norwich School	1096
10	Thetford Grammar School	1114

OLDEST UNIVERSITIES
in the UK

	University	Founded
1	Oxford	1117
2	Cambridge	1209
3	St Andrews	1411
4	Glasgow	1451
5	Aberdeen	1495
6	Edinburgh	1583
7	Dublin*	1592
8	Durham†	1832
9	London‡	1836
10	Manchester	1851

* Ireland then part of England
† A short-lived Cromwellian establishment was set up in 1657
‡ Constituent colleges were founded earlier: University College in 1826, King's College in 1828
Although its constituent colleges were founded earlier – Lampeter in 1822, Aberystwyth in 1872, Cardiff in 1883, Bangor in 1884 – the University of Wales dates from 1893.

TOP 10

SONGS PLAYED AT WEDDINGS
in the UK

	Song	Singer
1	'Amazed'	Lonestar
2	'Everything I Do (I Do it For You)'	Bryan Adams
3	'Angels'	Robbie Williams
4	'You're Beautiful'	James Blunt
5	'Don't Want To Miss a Thing'	Aerosmith
6	'Still The One'	Shania Twain
7	'Truly, Madly, Deeply'	Savage Garden
8	'Have I Told You Lately'	Van Morrison
9	'From This Moment On'	Shania Twain
10	'I Will Always Love You'	Whitney Houston

Source: Performing Right Society

SONGS REQUESTED AT FUNERALS
in the UK

	Song	Singer
1	'Goodbye My Lover'	James Blunt
2	'Angels'	Robbie Williams
3	'I've Had the Time of My Life'	Jennifer Warnes and Bill Medley
4	'Wind Beneath My Wings'	Bette Midler
5	'Pie Jesu'	from *Fauré's Requiem*
6	'Candle in the Wind'	Elton John
7	'With or Without You'	U2
8	'Tears in Heaven'	Eric Clapton
9	'Every Breath You Take'	The Police
10	'Unchained Melody'	Righteous Brothers

Source: The Bereavement Register

10
BRITONS WHOSE BODIES OR BODY PARTS have been separated

1 **Jeremy Bentham**
English philosopher Jeremy Bentham died aged 84 on 6 June 1832, having left instructions for his body to be publicly dissected and preserved in order to fulfil his plan for people to become their own memorials, or 'Auto-Icons'. This was carried out by Dr Thomas Southwood Smith, and since 1850 Bentham's seated body, dressed in his own clothes, has been kept in a glass-fronted case at University College London, although the poorly mummified head was replaced with a wax replica.

2 **Anne Boleyn**
Following her execution by sword on 19 May 1536, Henry VIII's second queen was buried at the Tower of London, but it is rumoured that her heart was taken to Elveden Park near Thetford, Norfolk, where it was found in 1836 and reburied at Salle Church – although several other locations have been claimed.

3 **Charles I**
Charles I was beheaded on 30 January 1649. When his tomb in Windsor Castle was opened on 1 April 1813, Sir Henry Halford, the royal doctor who examined the remains, took his fourth cervical vertebra – the one severed by the executioner's axe. It remained in his family as a conversation piece, but after Halford's death in 1844 was returned to the Royal Family for reburial.

4 **Edward II**
After his death – according to legend, murder with a red-hot poker – at Berkeley Castle, Gloucestershire, in 1327, Edward II was buried in St Peter's Abbey, later Gloucester Cathedral. His heart was removed, embalmed and placed in a silver urn and when Edward's queen Isabella died in 1358 she was buried at Greyfriars in London in the wedding gown she had worn in 1308, with Edward's heart on her chest.

5 **Oliver Cromwell**
Along with those of three other regicides, Oliver Cromwell's body was exhumed on 26 January 1661 and four days later, on the 12th anniversary of the execution of Charles I, his head was hacked off and displayed on a spike at Westminster Hall. It remained there until about 1685, falling in a storm, after which it changed hands several times, ending up with Canon Horace Wilkinson. It was finally laid to rest when, on 25 March 1960, it was secretly buried in the grounds of Sidney Sussex College, Cambridge.

6 John I

The English king was allegedly poisoned with toad venom, but probably died of dysentery at Newark, Nottinghamshire on 19 October 1216. His internal organs were sent to Croxton Abbey, Staffordshire, but his body, originally buried in Worcester Cathedral, was dug up, examined, and a portrait painted on 17 June 1797. At this time, two of his teeth were removed and are now displayed in Worcester City Art Gallery and Museum.

7 Benjamin Jonson

The British dramatist died on 6 August 1637. He was buried in a lead coffin in Westminster Abbey – standing up to economize on space, and with the inscription 'O Rare Ben Johnson' misspelling his name. In 1849, when an adjacent tomb was being dug for Sir Robert Wilson, Jonson's skeleton was dug up and his heelbone kept by William Buckland. It was last recorded in 1938, when it is said to have turned up in a furniture shop.

8 Sir Thomas More

After his beheading at the Tower of London on 6 July 1535, Thomas More's body was buried there at St Peter ad Vincula. His head was displayed on a spike on London Bridge until his daughter, Margaret Roper, acquired it and in 1544 it was buried with her at Chelsea. When her husband William died, Margaret's body and More's head were moved to the Roper family vault in St Dunstan's, Canterbury. The tomb was opened in 1824 and the head exhibited for several years.

9 Sir Walter Raleigh

The Elizabethan adventurer was executed at the Tower of London on 29 October 1618. His body was buried at St Margaret's, Westminster, but for the next 30 years his widow carried her husband's embalmed head with her in a red leather bag. Their son Carew followed the tradition, but after his death in 1666, the head was buried with him at St Mary's, West Horsley, Surrey.

10 Richard II

King Richard died imprisoned in Pontefract Castle in 1400 and was buried in Westminster Abbey. In 1776 a Westminster School schoolboy reached into the royal tomb and pulled out Richard's lower jawbone. It was promptly seized by a schoolmate, Gerrard Andrewes, whose descendants returned it in 1906.

10 UNUSUAL BRITISH EPITAPHS

1 ### Banbury, Oxfordshire
To the memory of Richard Richards
Who by gangrene lost first a Toe, afterwards a Leg
And lastly his Life
On the 7th day of April, 1656

2 ### Malmesbury Abbey
In memory of
Hannah Twynnoy
Who died October 23rd, 1703
Aged 33 Years.

In bloom of Life
She's snatch'd from hence
She had not room
To make defence;
For Tyger fierce
Took Life away.
And here she lies
In a bed of Clay,
Until the Resurrection Day.

Hannah was a barmaid who unwisely taunted a tiger in a travelling menagerie and was mauled to death.

3 ### Bunhill Fields, London
Here lies Dame Mary Page, relict [widow] of Sir Gregory Page, Bart. She departed this life March 4th, 1728, in the 56th year of her age. In 67 months she was tapped 66 times. Had taken away 240 gallons of water, without ever repining at her case, or ever fearing the operation.

4 ### Winchester Cathedral
In Memory of Thomas Thetcher, a Grenadier in the North Reg. of Hants Militia, who died of a violent Fever contracted by drinking Small Beer when hot the 12th of May 1764. Aged 26 Years.
Here sleeps in peace a Hampshire Grenadier,
Who caught his death by drinking cold small Beer,
Soldiers be wise from his untimely fall
And when ye're hot drink Strong or none at all.

5   Godalming, Surrey
Sacred
To the Memory of
Nathaniel Godbold, Esq.
Inventor and Proprietor
of that Excellent Medicine
The Vegetable Balsam
For the Cure of Consumption and Asthmas.
He departed this Life
The 17th Day of Decr., 1799
Aged 69 Years.
His ashes are here, his fame is everywhere.

6   St Mary, Lambeth, London
Sacred to the memory of Mr John Stevenson, late of this parish, who was unfortunately killed
by a stag at Astley's Amphitheatre, 6 Dec 1814 aged 49 years.

7   St Giles Burial Ground, London
In Memory of William Bingham, Surgeon to the Fever Hospital, Pancras Road, who departed
this life May 31st, 1821, aged 28 years. His death was occasioned by puncturing his finger while
sewing up a dead body.

8   St Mary with St Matthew, Cheltenham
Here lies John Higgs
A famous man for killing pigs,
For killing pigs was his delight
Both morning, afternoon and night
Both heats and cold he did endure
Which no Physician could e'er cure;
His knife is laid, his work is done,
I hope to heaven his soul is gone.

(John Higgs, pig-killer, died 26 November 1825.)

9   Hornsey, London
To the memory of
Emma and Maria Littleboy
The twin children of George and Emma Littleboy,
of Hornsey, who died July 16th, 1837

Two Littleboys lie here, yet strange to say
these Littleboys are girls.

10   St Lawrence, Reading, Berkshire
In memory of Henry West, who lost his life in a whirlwind at the Great Western Railway
Station, Reading, on the 24th of March 1840, aged 24 Years.

MOST COMMON CAUSES OF DEATH in the UK

	Cause	Deaths (2006) England and Wales	Scotland	Northern Ireland	UK total
1	Circulatory diseases	174,637	18,771	4,879	198,287
2	Cancer and other neoplasms	138,777	15,360	3,959	158,096
3	Diseases of the respiratory system	68,599	7,183	1,982	77,764
4	Diseases of the digestive system	25,786	3,208	646	29,640
5	External causes (accidents, suicide, murder, etc.)	17,509	2,237	853	20,599
6	Mental and behavioural disorders	14,863	2,817	418	18,098
7	Diseases of the nervous system and sense organs	15,218	1,333	557	17,108
8	Diseases of the genito-urinary system	10,722	1,112	359	12,193
9	Infectious and parasitic diseases	7,632	791	188	8,611
10	Endocrine, nutritional and metabolic diseases and immunity disorders	7,153	1,018	281	8,452
	Total deaths from all causes	*502,599*	*55,093*	*14,532*	*572,224*

ENTERTAINMENT

OLDEST THEATRES
in the UK

	Theatre	Opening show	Opened
1	Theatre Royal, Drury Lane, London	*The Humorous Lieutenant*	7 May 1663
2	Sadler's Wells, Rosebery Avenue, London	Musical performances	3 Jun 1683
3	The Haymarket (Theatre Royal), Haymarket, London	*La Fille à la Mode*	29 Dec 1720
4	Royal Opera House, Covent Garden, London	*The Way of the World*	7 Dec 1732
5	York Theatre Royal (founded as New Theatre; Royal from 1769)	*Henry V*	1744*
6	Theatre Royal, Bristol	*Concert of Music and a Specimen of Rhetorick*	30 May 1764
7	Grand Theatre, Lancaster	†	10 Jun 1782
8	Theatre Royal, Margate	*She Stoops to Conquer*	27 Jun 1787
9	Theatre Royal, Dumfries	*Othello*	29 Sep 1792
10	Theatre Royal, Bath	*Richard III*	12 Oct 1805

* Precise date unknown
† Opening show unknown; *Hamlet* performed in August 1782
These are Britain's 10 oldest theatres still operating on their original sites – although most of them have been rebuilt, some several times.

TOP 10
MOST-PRODUCED PLAYS
by Shakespeare

	Play	Productions
1	*As You Like It*	81
2=	*Hamlet*	80
=	*Twelfth Night*	80
4	*The Taming of the Shrew*	79
5	*A Midsummer-Night's Dream*	76
6	*Much Ado About Nothing*	72
7	*The Merchant of Venice*	70
8	*Macbeth*	67
9	*The Merry Wives of Windsor*	62
10	*Romeo and Juliet*	61

Source: Shakespeare Centre
This list is based on an analysis of Shakespearian productions (rather than individual performances) from 31 December 1878 to 31 December 2008 at Stratford-upon-Avon and by the Royal Shakespeare Company in London and on tour.

ANDREW LLOYD WEBBER
MUSICALS in London

	Show/run	Performances
1	*The Phantom of the Opera* (9 Oct 1986–)	9,000*
2	*Cats* (1981–2002)	8,949
3	*Starlight Express* (1984–2002)	7,406
4	*Jesus Christ Superstar* (1972–80)	3,358
5	*Evita* (1978–86)	2,900
6	*Sunset Boulevard* (1993–97)	1,529
7	*Aspects of Love* (1989–92)	1,325
8	*Whistle Down the Wind* (1998–2001)	1,044
9	*Song and Dance* (1982–84)	781
10	*Joseph and the Amazing Technicolor Dreamcoat* (2003–05)	768

* Still running, total as at 1 March 2008

LAURENCE OLIVIER FILMS

	Film	Year
1	*Clash of the Titans*	1981
2	*Spartacus*	1960
3	*Marathon Man*	1976
4	*The Jazz Singer*	1980
5	*Dracula*	1979
6	*The Betsy*	1978
7	*The Boys from Brazil*	1978
8	*Sleuth*	1972
9	*The Seven-Per-Cent Solution*	1976
10	*The Bounty*	1984

The voice of Laurence (Sir Laurence after 1947, Lord Olivier after 1970) was heard in *Romeo and Juliet* (1968), but was uncredited. If included, it would head this list.

RICHARD BURTON FILMS

	Film	Year
1	*Cleopatra*	1963
2	*The Longest Day*	1962
3	*The Robe*	1953
4	*Who's Afraid of Virginia Woolf?*	1966
5	*Exorcist II: The Heretic*	1977
6	*What's New, Pussycat?**	1965
7	*Candy*	1968
8	*Where Eagles Dare*	1969
9	*The Sandpiper*	1965
10	*Anne of the Thousand Days*	1969

* Uncredited
If Richard Burton's uncredited cameo role as a man at a bar in *What's New, Pussycat?* is discounted, *The VIPs* (1963) joins his Top 10.

AUDREY HEPBURN FILMS

	Film	Year
1	*My Fair Lady*	1964
2	*Always*	1989
3	*Wait until Dark*	1967
4	*Charade*	1963
5	*War and Peace*	1956
6	*The Nun's Story*	1959
7	*Bloodline*	1979
8	*How to Steal a Million*	1966
9	*Breakfast at Tiffany's*	1961
10=	*Sabrina*	1954
=	*Robin and Marian*	1976

Audrey Hepburn (born Edda van Heemstra Hepburn-Ruston, 4 May 1929, Brussels, Belgium; died 20 January 1993) had a British father and a Dutch mother. She began as a dancer and stage actress and appeared in minor parts before achieving acclaim and a Best Actress Oscar for *Roman Holiday* (1954). After 1967 her roles were few and far between, and her last years were devoted to charity work with UNICEF.

TOP 10

SEAN CONNERY FILMS

	Film	Year
1	*Indiana Jones and the Last Crusade*	1989
2	*The League of Extraordinary Gentlemen*	2003
3	*The Rock*	1996
4	*Entrapment*	1999
5	*The Hunt for Red October*	1990
6	*The Untouchables*	1987
7	*Thunderball*	1965
8	*Never Say Never Again*	1983
9	*First Knight*	1995
10	*Goldfinger*	1964

Every film in Sean Connery's Top 10 earned more than $100 million worldwide. His *James Bond* films occupy only three places, with a further three – *You Only Live Twice*, *From Russia with Love* and *Dr No* – outside it. If his fleeting cameo appearance as King Richard II in the final two minutes of *Robin Hood: Prince of Thieves* (1991) is taken into account, it would be placed second in the list. Sean Connery won his only Oscar for his supporting role in *The Untouchables*.

JAMES BOND FILMS
in the UK

	Film	Year	Total box-office gross*
1	*Casino Royale*	2006	£55,502,884
2	*Quantum of Solace*	2008	£45,120,024
3	*Die Another Day*	2002	£36,056,878
4	*The World is Not Enough*	1999	£28,576,504
5	*Tomorrow Never Dies*	1997	£19,884,412
6	*GoldenEye*	1995	£18,245,572
7	*For Your Eyes Only*	1981	£10,398,000
8	*Octopussy*	1983	£8,305,000
9	*The Living Daylights*	1987	£8,160,628
10	*Licence to Kill*	1989	£7,550,989

* As at 21 November 2008

TOP 10

FILMS DIRECTED BY ALFRED HITCHCOCK

	Film	Year
1	*Psycho*	1960
2	*Rear Window*	1954
3	*North by Northwest*	1959
4	*Family Plot*	1976
5	*Torn Curtain*	1966
6	*Frenzy*	1972
7	*The Birds*	1963
8	*The Man Who Knew Too Much*	1956
9	*Vertigo*	1958
10	*To Catch a Thief*	1955

London-born Alfred Hitchcock (1899–1980) directed over 50 films and is considered one of the most successful and influential directors of all time. All the films in his Top 10 earned upwards of $10 million, with *Psycho* taking some $32 million at the US box office alone. Despite being nominated for Best Director Oscars on five occasions, he never won an Oscar, but in 1968 was awarded the prestigious Irving G. Thalberg Memorial Award.

FILMS DIRECTED BY RIDLEY SCOTT

	Film	Year	Worldwide gross*
1	*Gladiator*	2000	$457,640,427
2	*Hannibal*	2001	$351,692,266
3	*American Gangster*	2007	$267,208,695
4	*Kingdom of Heaven*	2005	$211,652,051
5	*Black Hawk Down*	2001	$172,989,651
6	*Black Rain*	1989	$134,212,055
7	*Alien*	1979	$104,931,801
8	*G.I. Jane*	1997	$97,169,156
9	*Body of Lies*	2008	$71,053,891
10	*Matchstick Men*	2003	$65,565,672

* As at 21 November 2008

British director Sir Ridley Scott (b. South Shields, 1937) began his career in television and as a maker of such celebrated TV commercials as the 1974 Hovis bread advert filmed on Gold Hill, Shaftesbury, Dorset, once voted Britain's all-time favourite advertisement. He has been directing films since the late 1970s, with *The Duellists* (1977) and especially *Alien* (1979) and *Blade Runner* (1982) the start of a long run of box-office hits. He is credited with relaunching the epic 'sword and sandal' genre with the enormously successful *Gladiator* and *Kingdom of Heaven*. He has been nominated for an Oscar three times and was knighted in 2003.

BRITISH* FILMS
in the UK

	Film	Year	Total UK box-office gross†
1	*Mamma Mia!*	2008	£68,116,092
2	*Harry Potter and the Philosopher's Stone*	2001	£66,096,060
3	*Casino Royale*	2006	£55,502,884
4	*Harry Potter and the Chamber of Secrets*	2002	£54,780,731
5	*The Full Monty*	1997	£52,232,058
6	*Harry Potter and the Order of the Phoenix*	2007	£49,136,969
7	*Harry Potter and the Goblet of Fire*	2005	£48,769,962
8	*Harry Potter and the Prisoner of Azkaban*	2004	£46,077,489
9	*Quantum of Solace*	2008	£45,120,024
10	*The Chronicles of Narnia: The Lion, the Witch and the Wardrobe*	2005	£43,641,024

* Films with a significant British investment, production, British cast, etc.
† As at 21 November 2008

BESTSELLING DVDS
in the UK

1 *Pirates of the Caribbean: The Curse of the Black Pearl*

2 *The Lord of the Rings: The Fellowship of the Ring*

3 *The Lord of the Rings: The Two Towers*

4 *Pirates of the Caribbean: Dead Man's Chest*

5 *The Lord of the Rings: The Return of the King*

6 *Shrek 2*

7 *The Shawshank Redemption*

8 *Gladiator*

9 *Casino Royale*

10 *Harry Potter and the Goblet of Fire*

Source: British Video Association/The Official UK Charts Company
The 1999 release of *The Shawshank Redemption* marks it out as the earliest DVD in this all-time list. Later releases have benefited from the progressive increase in DVD market penetration: it is estimated that while some 25 per cent of UK homes owned a DVD player in 2002, this figure grew to 86 per cent in 2007.

TOP 10

LONGEST-RUNNING PROGRAMMES
on BBC Radio

	Programme	First broadcast
1	*The Week's Good Cause*	24 Jan 1926
2	*The Shipping Forecast*	26 Jan 1926
3	*Choral Evensong*	7 Oct 1926
4	*Daily Service*	2 Jan 1928*
5	*The Week in Westminster*	6 Nov 1929
6	*Sunday Half Hour*	14 Jul 1940
7	*Desert Island Discs*	29 Jan 1942
8	*Saturday Night Theatre*	3 Apr 1943
9	*Composer of the Week†*	2 Aug 1943
10	*From Our Own Correspondent*	4 Oct 1946

* Experimental broadcast; national transmission began December 1929
† Formerly *This Week's Composer*
In addition to these 10 long-running programmes, a further six that started in the 1940s are still on the air, with *Woman's Hour*, first broadcast on 7 October 1946, and *Down Your Way* (29 December 1946) the oldest.

LONGEST-RUNNING PROGRAMMES
on British television

	Programme	First broadcast
1	*Panorama*	11 Nov 1953
2	*What the Papers Say*	5 Nov 1956
3	*The Sky at Night*	24 Apr 1957
4	*Blue Peter*	16 Oct 1958
5	*Coronation Street*	9 Dec 1960
6	*Songs of Praise*	1 Oct 1961
7	*Horizon*	2 May 1964
8	*Match of the Day*	22 Aug 1964
9	*The Money Programme*	5 Apr 1966
10	*Gardeners' World*	5 Jan 1968

Only programmes appearing every year since their first screenings are listed. *The Queen's Christmas Message* began broadcasting in sound only in 1952 and in vision from 1957, but as it was not broadcast in 1969, it has not had a continuous run. All those in the Top 10 are BBC programmes except *Coronation Street*. The first nine programmes predate the colour era. *The Sky at Night* has the additional distinction of having had the same presenter, Patrick Moore, since its first programme.

THE 10
LATEST *MASTERMIND* CHAMPIONS

Champion/broadcaster

2008   David Clark (BBC)
Subjects: The life and career of Henry Ford; The Prince Regent, later King George IV; The history of London Bridge

2006   Geoff Thomas (BBC)
Subjects: Edith Piaf; William Joyce; Margaret Mitchell

2005   Patrick Gibson (BBC)
Subjects: The films of Quentin Tarantino; The novels of Iain M. Banks; *Father Ted*

2004   Shaun Wallace (BBC)
Subjects: The History of the European Cup Finals since 1970; The England Football Team at the European Championships 1960–2003; FA Cup Finals since 1970

2003   Andy Page (BBC)
Subjects: The Academy Awards; The life and works of Gilbert and Sullivan; Golfing Majors since 1970

2001   Michael Penrice (Discovery Channel)
Subjects: Professional boxing to 1980; (no semi-final); English history 1603–1714

2000   Stephen Follows (BBC Radio 4)
Subjects: The life and operas of Benjamin Britten; The poetry and plays of T. S. Eliot; The life and operas of Leoš Janáček

1999   Rev. Christopher 'Kit' Carter (BBC Radio 4)
Subjects: The birds of Europe; The House of Tudor; The customs and traditions of Great Britain

1998   Robert Gibson (BBC Radio 4)
Subjects: The Solar System; Charles II; Robert the Bruce

1997   Anne Ashurst (BBC)
Subjects: Frances Howard, Countess of Somerset; The Regency novels of Georgette Heyer; Barbara Villiers, Duchess of Cleveland

There were no contests in 2002 and 2007.

TOP 10

SINGLES
in the UK

	Title/artist/year	Estimated sales
1	'Candle in the Wind'/'Something About the Way You Look Tonight', Elton John, 1997	4,864,611
2	'Do They Know It's Christmas?', Band Aid, 1984	3,550,000
3	'Bohemian Rhapsody', Queen, 1975/91	2,130,000
4	'Mull of Kintyre', Wings, 1977	2,050,000
5	'Rivers of Babylon'/'Brown Girl in the Ring', Boney M, 1978	1,985,000
6	'You're the One That I Want', John Travolta and Olivia Newton-John, 1978	1,975,000
7	'Relax', Frankie Goes to Hollywood, 1984	1,910,000
8	'She Loves You', The Beatles, 1963	1,890,000
9	'Unchained Melody', Robson Green and Jerome Flynn, 1995	1,843,701
10=	'Mary's Boy Child'/'Oh My Lord', Boney M, 1978	1,790,000
=	'Anything Is Possible'/'Evergreen', Will Young, 2002	1,790,000

Source: The Official UK Charts Company
Seventy-nine singles have sold over a million copies apiece in the UK during the last 50 years, and these are the cream of that crop. The Band Aid single had a host of special circumstances surrounding it, and it took the remarkable response to the death of Diana, Princess of Wales, to overtake it. Two years, 1978 and 1984, were the all-time strongest for million-selling singles, and this chart fittingly has three representatives from each, though the only act to appear twice is Boney M, a group masterminded by German producer Frank Farian (aka Frank Reuther). They had a string of UK chart singles, but no others ever came close to the sales figures achieved by their two 1978 mega-hits.

CHRISTMAS SINGLES
in the UK

	Title/artist	Year of highest chart position
1	'White Christmas', Bing Crosby	1977
2	'Do They Know It's Christmas?', Band Aid	1984
3	'Mary's Boy Child'/'Oh My Lord', Boney M	1978
4	'Last Christmas', Wham!	1984
5	'Mary's Boy Child', Harry Belafonte	1957
6	'Do They Know It's Christmas?', Band Aid	2004
7	'Merry Xmas Everybody', Slade	1973
8	'Do They Know It's Christmas?', Band Aid	1990
9	'Mistletoe and Wine', Cliff Richard	1988
10	'When a Child is Born', Johnny Mathis	1976

Source: Music Information Database

On occasions the annual battle for Britain's Christmas No.1 has been won by a Christmas-themed single, of which these are the bestselling. Bing Crosby's 'White Christmas,' taken from the film *Holiday Inn* (1942), is claimed to have sold more than 30 million copies worldwide, making it the bestselling single ever, but it charted for the first time in the UK as late as 1977, a few weeks after the singer's death. Band Aid's 'Do They Know It's Christmas?' has now sold over 3,550,000 copies in the UK alone.

ONE-HIT-WONDER SINGLES
in the UK*

	Title/artist	Year of chart entry
1	'Do They Know It's Christmas?', Band Aid	1984
2	'Do They Know It's Christmas?', Band Aid	2004
3	'Teletubbies Say Eh-Oh!', Teletubbies	1997
4	'The Ketchup Song (Asereje)', Las Ketchup	2002
5	'Eye Level' (theme from TV series *Van der Valk*), Simon Park Orchestra	1973
6	'Sugar Sugar', Archies	1969
7	'Grandad', Clive Dunn	1971
8	'Mad World', Michael Andrews, featuring Gary Jules	2003
9	'Flat Beat', Mr Oizo	1999
10	'Amazing Grace', Pipes and Drums and the Military Band of the Royal Scots Dragoon Guards (Carabiniers and Greys)	1972

* Ranked by sales
Source: Music Information Database

TOP 10

HIGHEST-SCORING
British Eurovision Song Contest entries

	Singer	Song	Year	Place	Points
1	Katrina & the Waves	'Love Shine a Light'	1997	1	227
2	Imaani	'Where Are You?'	1998	2	166
3=	Brotherhood of Man	'Save Your Kisses for Me'	1976	1	164
=	Sonia	'Better the Devil You Know'	1993	2	164
5	Michael Ball	'One Step Out of Time'	1992	2	139
6	Shadows	'Let Me Be the One'	1975	2	138
7=	Bucks Fizz	'Making Your Mind Up'	1981	1	136
=	Scott Fitzgerald	'Go'	1988	2	136
9	Live Report	'Why Do I Always Get It Wrong?'	1989	2	130
10	Cliff Richard	'Power to All Our Friends'	1973	3	123

THE 10
LOWEST-SCORING
British Eurovision Song Contest entries

	Singer	Song	Year	Place	Points
1	Jemini	'Cry Baby'	2003	26	0
2	Patricia Bredin	'All'	1957	7	6
3	Kenneth McKellar	'A Man Without Love'	1966	9	8
4	Ronnie Carroll	'Ring-a-Ding Girl'	1962	4	10
5=	Olivia Newton-John	'Long Live Love'	1974	4	14
=	Andy Abraham	'Even If'	2008	25	14
7	Pearl Carr and Teddy Johnson	'Sing, Little Birdie'	1959	2	16
8	Matt Monro	'I Love the Little Things'	1964	2	17
9=	Lulu	'Boom Bang-a-Bang'	1969	1	18
=	Javine	'Touch My Fire'	2005	22	18

These figures should be interpreted with caution. Since the inaugural Eurovision Song Contest in 1956, the number of participating countries and the method of scoring have changed, so that Lulu, for example, with the ninth score here, actually won the contest that year.

FIRST ACTS TO PERFORM AT LIVE AID, 1985

	Act	Opening number
1	Status Quo	'Rockin' All Over the World'
2	Style Council (Paul Weller)	'You're the Best Thing'
3	Boomtown Rats (Bob Geldof)	'I Don't Like Mondays'
4	Adam Ant	'Vive le Rock'
5	Ultravox	'Reap the Wild Wind'
6	Spandau Ballet	'Only When You Leave'
7	Elvis Costello	'All You Need is Love'
8	Shahrouz Homavaran	'Children Need to Have Home'
9	Nik Kershaw	'Wide Boy'
10	Sade	'Why Can't We Live Together'

After a royal salute and 'God Save the Queen' played by the band of the Coldstream Guards, Status Quo took the stage at Wembley Stadium at midday on 13 July 1985 to begin the historic 16-hour fund-raising rock extravaganza, Live Aid. The event was broadcast live to an estimated 1.5–2 billion people around the world from the two principal venues, Wembley and the JFK Stadium, Philadelphia, USA (there were small-scale events in Melbourne and other cities on the same day), and raised over $70 million for famine relief in Africa. Phil Collins made rock history by playing a set at Wembley, flying immediately to Philadelphia by Concorde and performing a second set in the States, the first time an artist had ever played two gigs on different continents on the same day.

SINGLES IN THE UK
banned by the BBC

	Title/artist	Year
1	'Relax', Frankie Goes to Hollywood	1983
2	'Je t'aime … moi non plus', Jane Birkin and Serge Gainsbourg	1969
3	'Tell Laura I Love Her', Ricky Valance	1960
4	'God Save the Queen', Sex Pistols	1977
5	'I Want Your Sex', George Michael	1987
6	'Love to Love You Baby', Donna Summer	1976
7	'Magic Roundabout', Jasper Carrott	1975
8	'Hi Hi Hi', Wings	1972
9	'Wet Dream', Max Romeo	1969
10	'Big Seven', Judge Dread	1972

Source: Music Information Database
Until recent years, BBC radio was prone to keep records off the airwaves if (a) their melody was a desecration of a classical piece (though, oddly, 'Nut Rocker' never succumbed), (b) their lyrics were deemed offensive because of a concern with sex, drugs, death or politics, or (c) they mentioned commercial trade names, which was reckoned to be against the BBC's charter. Most of those on the list were adjudged to be in category (b) – and yet they all became Top 10 hits regardless. (A sign of the changing times: George Michael's disc was banned only from daytime play, but permitted after the 9 p.m. 'watershed'.)

TOP 10

ALBUMS
in the UK

	Title/artist/year	Sales
1	*Greatest Hits*, Queen (1981)	5,407,587
2	*Sgt Pepper's Lonely Hearts Club Band*, The Beatles (1967)	4,803,292
3	*(What's the Story) Morning Glory*, Oasis (1995)	4,303,504
4	*Brothers in Arms*, Dire Straits (1985)	3,946,931
5	*Abba Gold Greatest Hits*, Abba (1990)	3,932,316
6	*The Dark Side of the Moon*, Pink Floyd (1973)	3,759,958
7	*Greatest Hits II*, Queen (1991)	3,631,321
8	*Thriller*, Michael Jackson (1982)	3,570,250
9	*Bad*, Michael Jackson (1987)	3,549,950
10	*The Immaculate Collection*, Madonna (1990)	3,364,785

Source: The Official UK Charts Company

TOP 10
BEATLES ALBUMS
in the UK

	Title	Year
1	*Sgt Pepper's Lonely Hearts Club Band*	1967
2	*1*	2000
3	*Abbey Road*	1969
4	*Beatles for Sale*	1964
5	*A Hard Day's Night*	1964
6	*Rubber Soul*	1965
7	*Revolver*	1966
8	*Anthology 1*	1995
9	*Love*	2006
10	*Live at the BBC*	1995

Source: Music Information Database

TOP 10

ROLLING STONES ALBUMS
in the UK

	Title	Year
1	*Forty Licks*	2002
2	*Jump Back – The Best of the Rolling Stones*	1993
3	*Hot Licks 1964–1971*	1990
4	*Let It Bleed*	1969
5	*Big Hits (High Tide and Green Grass)*	1966
6	*The Rolling Stones*	1964
7	*Rolled Gold*	1975
8	*Through the Past Darkly (Big Hits Vol. 2)*	1969
9	*Rolling Stones No. 2*	1965
10	*Aftermath*	1966

Source: Music Information Database

KARAOKE SONGS
in the UK

	Song	Singer
1	'Angels'	Robbie Williams
2	'Summer Nights'	John Travolta & Olivia Newton-John
3	'Paradise by the Dashboard Light'	Meat Loaf
4	'My Way'	Frank Sinatra
5	'Mustang Sally'	The Commitments
6	'I Will Survive'	Gloria Gaynor
7	'Words'	Boyzone
8	'Suspicious Minds'	Elvis Presley
9	'Build Me Up Buttercup'	The Foundations
10	'Mack The Knife'	Bobby Darin

Source: www.karaokeinfo.co.uk

OPERAS MOST FREQUENTLY PERFORMED at the Royal Opera House

	Opera	Composer	First performance	Total*
1	*La Bohème*	Giacomo Puccini	2 Oct 1897	569
2	*Carmen*	Georges Bizet	27 May 1882	519
3	*Aïda*	Giuseppe Verdi	22 Jun 1876	481
4	*Rigoletto*	Giuseppe Verdi	14 May 1853	471
5	*Faust*	Charles Gounod	18 Jul 1863	448
6	*Tosca*	Giacomo Puccini	12 Jul 1900	442
7	*Don Giovanni*	Wolfgang Amadeus Mozart	17 Apr 1834	434
8	*La Traviata*	Giuseppe Verdi	25 May 1858	421
9	*Madama Butterfly*	Giacomo Puccini	10 Jul 1905	387
10	*Le Nozze di Figaro*	Wolfgang Amadeus Mozart	6 Mar 1819	360

* To 31 December 2008

Most of the works listed were first performed at Covent Garden within a few years of their world premieres (in the case of *Tosca*, in the same year). Although some were considered controversial at the time, all of them are now regarded as important components of the classic opera repertoire.

THE
QUEEN'S
ENGLISH

TOP 10
MOST COMMON WORDS
in English

	Word	Frequency
1	the	6,187,267
2	of	2,941,444
3	and	2,682,863
4	a	2,126,369
5	in	1,812,609
6	to	1,620,850
7	it	1,089,186
8	is	998,389
9	was	923,948
10	to	917,579

The British National Corpus surveys a wide range of written texts and spoken examples, with these representing the most commonly used among 100,106,029 words across both categories. The most common noun is 'time', the most common verb 'be', the most common adjective 'other' and the most common adverb 'so'. In spoken English, interjections such as 'yeah' and 'oh' appear in the Top 20.

MOST COMMONLY MISSPELLED
English words

	Word	Percentage misspelled
1	minuscule	68
2	millennium	57
3	embarrassment	55
	embarrassing	*35*
4=	occurrence	44
	occurring	*37*
=	superseded	44
	supersede	*35*
6	accommodate	40
	accommodation	*39*
7	perseverance	36
8	noticeable	35
9=	harass	34
=	inoculate	34

Based on a survey by spelling expert Cornell Kimball of instances where a word was misspelled on Internet newsgroup posts.

CLICHÉS COINED BY SHAKESPEARE

1 **All Greek to me** (*Julius Caesar* I.ii)
Casca, in *Julius Caesar* describes hearing a speech by the orator, Cicero – but as Cicero spoke in Greek, he did not understand it and comments, '...it was Greek to me.'

2 **Be-all and end-all** (*Macbeth* I.vii)
Macbeth muses on the assassination of Duncan, describing its potential significance as '...the be-all and end-all.'

3 **The course of true love never did run smooth** (*A Midsummer-Night's Dream* I.i)
Hermia is being pressed into marriage with Demetrius, rather than Lysander whom she loves. In an attempt to comfort her, Lysander tells Hermia, 'The course of true love never did run smooth.'

4 **Eaten me out of house and home** (*Henry IV* II.ii)
Mistress Quickly complains that the gluttonous Sir John Falstaff '...hath eaten me out of house and home.'

5 **A foregone conclusion** (*Othello* III.iii)
Cassio has been talking in his sleep. Iago relates this to Othello, dismissing it as just a dream. 'But this denoted a foregone conclusion,' Othello responds.

6 **For ever and a day** (*As You Like It* IV.i)
Meeting him in the Forest of Arden, Rosalind asks Orlando how long he expects to stay with her – 'For ever and a day,' he answers. The same line appears in *The Taming of the Shrew* (IV.iv), when Biondello tells Lucentio, '...bid Bianca farewell for ever and a day.'

7 **Gild the lily** (*King John* IV.ii)
Referring to the fact that King John has had two coronations, the Earl of Salisbury remarks that this 'double pomp' can be compared with other extravagant displays, such as, 'To gild refined gold, to paint the lily.'

8 **Laid on with a trowel** (*As You Like It* I.ii)
Celia in *As You Like It* replies to a flattering remark with, 'Well said: that was laid on with a trowel.'

9 Murder most foul (*Hamlet* I.v)

The ghost of Hamlet's father appears to him and reveals the circumstances of his death, describing his poisoning at the hand of his brother, Claudius, as 'Murder most foul' – a cliché that has since been much used, especially by thriller writers.

10 A pound of flesh (*The Merchant of Venice* I.iii)

In *The Merchant of Venice*, Antonio's pledge of a pound of his flesh to Shylock, the money-lender, is regarded as a jest – until Shylock insists on being paid according to the letter of the law; the phrase, 'a pound of flesh' is used no fewer than nine times in the play.

William Shakespeare (1564–1616) is the most-quoted author in the English language. The words and phrases used by him in his 38 plays and poems are the most cited of any author in the *Oxford English Dictionary*, a total of 33,303 – more than twice as many as the next most quoted, Sir Walter Scott, and four times as many as Charles Dickens. Many of the phrases he coined have entered the language, becoming widely used clichés. In addition to those above, Shakespeare gave us 'Cold comfort' (*King John*), 'A fool's paradise' (*Romeo and Juliet*), 'Milk of human kindness' (*Macbeth*), 'A tower of strength' (*Richard III*), 'All the world's a stage' (*As You Like It*), 'Dead as a doornail' (*Henry VI, part 2*), 'For goodness sake' (*Henry VIII*) and 'Good riddance' (*Troilus and Cressida*). Some, such as 'Brave new world' (*The Tempest*) and 'Pomp and Circumstance' (*Othello*) have been used as the titles of books and orchestral works, so making them even more familiar.

10 UNUSUAL REGIONAL WORDS

	Word	**Region**
1	**bowssen** To immerse or duck an insane person in a holy well	Cornwall
2	**flurn** To show contempt for, or scorn	Lincolnshire
3	**guddle** To catch trout by hand	Scotland and Northumberland
4	**hotagoe** To speak quickly or babble	Sussex
5	**mouldy-band** An anthill	Northamptonshire
6	**peever** The stone or pottery used in playing hopscotch	Scotland
7	**slench** To prune one side of a hedge	Cheshire
8	**snurl** A cold in the head	Suffolk
9	**twink** A sharp or shrewish woman	Kent
10	**wimble-wamble** A rolling style of walking	Gloucestershire

BRITISH TV CATCHPHRASES

1 'I don't believe it'
   Victor Meldrew (Richard Wilson), *One Foot in the Grave*

2 'Yeah, but, no, but . . .'
   Vicky Pollard (Matt Lucas), *Little Britain*

3 'Lovely jubbly'
   Del Boy (David Jason), *Only Fools and Horses*

4 'Am I bovvered?'
   Lauren Cooper (Catherine Tate), *The Catherine Tate Show*

5 'I'm a laydee'
   Emily (Eddie) Howard (David Walliams), *Little Britain*

6 'Deal or no deal?'
   Noel Edmonds, *Deal or No Deal*

7 'Here's one I made earlier'
   Various presenters, *Blue Peter*

8 'Suit you, sir'
   Ken (Paul Whitehouse) and Kenneth (Mark Williams), *The Fast Show*

9 'I'm the only gay in the village'
   Dafydd Thomas (Matt Lucas), *Little Britain*

10 'Just like that'
   Tommy Cooper

Source: www.onepoll.com survey, 2008

FIRST PUBLICATIONS
printed in England

Author/publication

1 *Propositio ad Carolum ducem Burgundiae*

2 Cato, *Disticha de Morbidus*

3 Geoffrey Chaucer, *The Canterbury Tales*

4 *Ordinale seu Pica ad usem Sarum* ('*Sarum Pie*')

5 John Lydgate, *The Temple of Glass*

6 John Lydgate, *Stans puer mensam*

7 John Lydgate, *The Horse, the Sheep and the Goose*

8 John Lydgate, *The Churl and the Bird*

9 *Infanta Salvatoris*

10 William Caxton, advertisement for '*Sarum Pie*'

Source: British Library
All the first known publications in England were printed by William Caxton (*c.*1422–*c.*1491) at Westminster. He had previously printed books in Bruges, where in about 1474 he printed the first book in English, *Recuyell of the Historyes of Troye*, followed by *The Game and Playe of the Chesse*. He then moved to England, where *Propositio ad Carolum ducem Burgundiae* was printed some time before September 1476; the others were all printed at unknown dates in either 1476 or 1477. It is probable that Chaucer's *Canterbury Tales* was the first book in English to be printed in England.

ORIGINAL TITLES OF CLASSIC BRITISH BOOKS

1   *First Impressions*
    Published title: *Pride and Prejudice,* Jane Austen (1813)

2   *Prometheus Unchained; Victor Frankenstein*
    Published title: *Frankenstein,* Mary Shelley (1818)

3   *Tom-All-Alone's Factory that Got into Chancery and Never
    Got Out; The Ruined House; The East Wind*
    Published title: *Bleak House,* Charles Dickens, (1853)

4   *The Body and Soul of Sue; Too Late, Beloved; Tess of the Hardys*
    Published title: *Tess of the d'Urbervilles,* Thomas Hardy (1891)

5   *The Sea-Cook*
    Published title: *Treasure Island,* Robert Louis Stevenson (1883)

6   *The Mole and the Water-Rat*
    Published title: *The Wind in the Willows,* Kenneth Grahame (1908)

7   *Tenderness*
    Published title: *Lady Chatterley's Lover,* D. H. Lawrence (1928)

8   *House of Faith*
    Published title: *Brideshead Revisited,* Evelyn Waugh (1945)

9   *The Last Man in Europe*
    Published title: *Nineteen Eighty-Four,* George Orwell (1949)

10 *Harry Potter and the Doomspell Tournament; Harry Potter and the
    Triwizard Tournament*
    Published title: *Harry Potter and the Goblet of Fire,* J. K. Rowling (2000)

OPENINGS OF CLASSIC BRITISH BOOKS

1 Daniel Defoe, *Robinson Crusoe*, 1719
   'I was born in the year 1632, in the city of York, of a good family, though not of that country, my father being a foreigner of Bremen, who settled first at Hull.'

2 Jane Austen, *Pride and Prejudice*, 1813
   'It is a truth universally acknowledged, that a single man in possession of a good fortune, must be in want of a wife.'

3 Charlotte Brontë, *Jane Eyre*, 1847
   'There was no possibility of taking a walk that day.'

4 Charles Dickens, *A Tale of Two Cities*, 1859
   'It was the best of times, it was the worst of times, it was the age of wisdom, it was the age of foolishness...'

5 Lewis Carroll, *Alice's Adventures in Wonderland*, 1865
   'Alice was beginning to get very tired of sitting by her sister on the bank and of having nothing to do: once or twice she had peeped into the book her sister was reading, but it had no pictures or conversations in it, "and what is the use of a book," thought Alice, "without pictures or conversations?"'

6 J. M. Barrie, *Peter Pan in Kensington Gardens*, 1906
   'All children, except one, grow up. They soon know that they will grow up, and the way Wendy knew was this.'

7 Kenneth Grahame, *The Wind in the Willows*, 1908
   'The Mole had been working very hard all the morning, spring-cleaning his little home.'

8 D. H. Lawrence, *Lady Chatterley's Lover*, 1928
   'Ours is essentially a tragic age, so we refuse to take it tragically.'

9 George Orwell, *Nineteen Eighty-Four*, 1949
   'It was a bright cold day in April, and the clocks were striking thirteen.'

10 L. P. Hartley, *The Go-Between*, 1953
   'The past is a foreign country: they do things differently there.'

ENDINGS OF CLASSIC BRITISH BOOKS

1 John Milton, *Paradise Lost* (1667)
'They hand in hand with wandring steps and slow, Through Eden took thir solitarie way.'

2 Lawrence Sterne, *The Life and Opinions of Tristram Shandy, Gentleman* (1759–67)
'"Lord!" said my mother, "what is all this story about?"
"A Cock and a Bull," said Yorick – "And one of the best of its kind, I ever heard."'

3 Jane Austen, *Pride and Prejudice* (1813)
'Darcy, as well as Elizabeth, really loved them; and they were both ever sensible of the warmest gratitude towards the persons who, by bringing her into Derbyshire, had been the means of uniting them.'

4 Emily Brontë, *Wuthering Heights* (1847)
'I … listened to the soft wind breathing through the grass, and wondered how any one could ever imagine unquiet slumbers for the sleepers in that quiet earth.'

5 William Makepeace Thackeray, *Vanity Fair* (1848)
'Which of us is happy in this world? Which of us has his desire? or, having it, is satisfied? – come, children, let us shut up the box and the puppets, for our play is played out.'

6 Charles Dickens, *A Tale of Two Cities* (1859)
'It is a far, far better thing that I do, than I have ever done; it is a far, far better rest that I go to than I have ever known.'

7 Thomas Hardy, *Tess of the D'Urbervilles* (1891)
'The two speechless gazers bent themselves down to the earth, as if in prayer, and remained thus a long time, absolutely motionless: the flag continued to wave silently. As soon as they had strength, they arose, joined hands again, and went on.'

8 Evelyn Waugh, *Vile Bodies* (1930)
'And presently, like a circling typhoon, the sounds of battle began to return.'

9 George Orwell, *Animal Farm* (1945)
'The creatures outside looked from pig to man, and from man to pig, and from pig to man again; but already it was impossible to say which was which.'

10 Douglas Adams, *The Hitch Hiker's Guide to the Galaxy* (1979)
'"We'll take in a quick bite at the Restaurant at the End of the Universe."'

MISTAKES BY GREAT BRITISH WRITERS

1   William Shakespeare, *The Winter's Tale* (1623)
Shakespeare refers to a ship 'driven by storm on the coast of Bohemia' and refers to the country's desert. Bohemia – roughly synonymous with today's Czech Republic – is land-locked and has no desert.

2   Daniel Defoe, *Robinson Crusoe* (1719)
After swimming to the shipwreck naked, Crusoe fills his pockets with biscuits.

3   Samuel Johnson, *A Dictionary of the English Language* (1755)
Johnson defined a pastern as 'the knee of a horse' (it is actually the part of a horse's leg between the fetlock and hoof). When questioned about it by a woman, Johnson explained his mistake as 'Ignorance, madam, sheer ignorance'.

4   Oliver Goldsmith, *The History of England* (1789)
Goldsmith states that Naseby, the site of the celebrated Civil War battle of 1645, is in Yorkshire. It is in Northamptonshire.

5   Jane Austen, *Love and Freindship* (1790)
The story Jane Austen wrote at the age of 14 misspelled 'Friendship' in the title.

6   John Keats, 'On First Looking into Chapman's Homer' (1816)
In Keats's poem, Cortez, 'Silent, upon a peak in Darien', discovers the Pacific. Not only is the Pacific not visible from Darien, but it was Vasco Núñez de Balboa, not Cortez, who established Santa María la Antigua del Darién in 1510.

7   Sir Walter Scott, *Ivanhoe* (1819)
The first name of the character introduced as Richard de Malvoisin changes during the story to Philip.

8   Charles Dickens, *Bleak House* (1853)
Harold Skimpole turns into Leonard and back again.

9   H. Rider Haggard, *King Solomon's Mines* (1885)
Haggard described a full moon, a total eclipse of the sun and another full moon on succes-sive days. When he realized his error, he changed the solar eclipse into a lunar one.

10   Arthur Conan Doyle, *A Study in Scarlet* (1887)
Sherlock Holmes's companion Dr Watson has a war wound to his shoulder in this, the first book in which he appears, but in *The Sign of the Four* (1890) it migrates to his leg. Watson himself is variously called John and James.

BIZARRE BRITISH BOOKS

1   *Premature Burial and How It May Be Prevented*
William Tebb and Col. Edward Perry Vollum (London: Swan Sonnenschein & Co., 1896)

2   *Octogenarian Teetotalers, with One Hundred and Thirteen Portraits*
Anon. (London: National Temperance League Publication Depot, 1897)

3   *A Study of Splashes*
Arthur Mason Worthington (London: Longmans, Green, 1908)

4   *Jokes Cracked by Lord Aberdeen*
Lord Aberdeen (John Campbell Gordon) (Dundee: Valentine, 1929)

5   *Fish Who Answer the Telephone*
Yury Petrovich Frolov (London: Kegan Paul, Trench, Trübner, 1937)

6   *The Fangs of Suet Pudding*
Adams Farr (London: Gerald G. Swan, 1944)

7   *The Romance of Leprosy*
E. Mackerchar (London: The Mission to Lepers, 1949)

8   *Hot Wireless Sets, Aspirin Tablets, the Sandpaper Sides of Used Matchboxes, and Something That Might Have Been Castor Oil*
D. G. Compton (London: Michael Joseph, 1971)

9   *Searching for Railway Telegraph Insulators*
W. Keith Neal (St Saviours, Guernsey: The Signal Box Press, 1982)

10 *By His Own Hand: A Study of Cricket's Suicides*
David Frith (London: Stanley Paul, 1991)

TOP 10

BESTSELLING BRITISH BOOKS

	Book	Estimated sales
1	Thomas Cranmer, *Book of Common Prayer* (1549)	300,000,000
2	John Bunyan, *The Pilgrim's Progress* (1678)	250,000,000
3	John Foxe, *Foxe's Book of Martyrs* (1563)	150,000,000
4	J. K. Rowling, *Harry Potter and the Philosopher's Stone* (1997)	117,000,000
5	Agatha Christie, *And Then There Were None* (1939)	110,000,000
6	J. R. R. Tolkien, *The Lord of the Rings* (1954–5)	100,000,000
7	J. K. Rowling, *Harry Potter and the Chamber of Secrets* (1998)	77,000,000
8	J. K. Rowling, *Harry Potter and the Goblet of Fire* (2000)	66,000,000
9	J. K. Rowling, *Harry Potter and the Half-Blood Prince* (2005)	65,000,000
10	J. K. Rowling, *Harry Potter and the Order of the Phoenix* (2003)	58,000,000

LATEST WINNERS OF
the Man Booker Prize

	Author	Title
2008	Aravind Adiga	*The White Tiger*
2007	Anne Enright	*The Gathering*
2006	Kiran Desai	*The Inheritance of Loss*
2005	John Banville	*The Sea*
2004	Alan Hollinghurst	*The Line of Beauty*
2003	D. B. C. Pierre	*Vernon God Little*
2002	Yann Martel	*Life of Pi*
2001	Peter Carey	*True History of the Kelly Gang*
2000	Margaret Atwood	*The Blind Assassin*
1999	J. M. Coetzee	*Disgrace*

LONGEST-SERVING POETS LAUREATE

	Poet	In office	Years	Duration Months	Days
1	Alfred, Lord Tennyson	19 Nov 1850–6 Oct 1892	41	10	17
2	John Masefield	9 May 1930–12 May 1967	37	0	3
3	Robert Southey	? Oct 1813–21 Mar 1843*	30	?	?
4	William Whitehead	19 Dec 1757–14 Apr 1785	27	3	26
5	Colley Cibber	3 Dec 1730–12 Dec 1757	27	0	9
6	Nahum Tate	8 Dec 1692–30 Jul 1715	22	7	22
7	Henry James Pye	28 Jul 1790–11 Aug 1813	23	0	14
8	John Dryden	13 Apr 1668–1689* (stripped)	20	?	?
9	Alfred Austin	1 Jan 1896–2 Jun 1913	17	5	1
10	Robert Bridges	16 Jul 1913–21 Apr 1930	16	9	5

* Precise date unknown
Dryden was stripped of his laureateship after James II was deposed (11 December 1688) and he refused to swear allegiance to William III; he was replaced in early 1689 (date unknown) by Thomas Shadwell.

MOST POPULAR BRITISH POEMS

Poem	Poet
1 'If'	Rudyard Kipling (1865–1936)
2 'The Lady of Shallot'	Alfred, Lord Tennyson (1809–92)
3 'The Listeners'	Walter de la Mare (1873–1956)
4 'Not Waving but Drowning'	Stevie Smith (1902–71)
5 'Daffodils'	William Wordsworth (1770–1850)
6 'To Autumn'	John Keats (1795–1821)
7 'The Lake Isle of Innisfree'	W. B. Yeats (1864–1939)
8 'Dulce et Decorum'	Wilfred Owen (1893–1918)
9 'Ode to a Nightingale'	John Keats (1795–1821)
10 'He Wishes for the Cloths of Heaven'	W. B. Yeats (1864–1939)

In a survey conducted by telephone during the six days leading up to the UK's National Poetry Day on 12 October 1995, more than 1,000 poems by over 200 authors were nominated. Bookmakers Ladbrokes had laid odds of 2/1 that Shakespeare's Sonnet XVIII ('Shall I compare thee to a summer's day?') would win, but in the event the Bard, along with other favourites such as William Blake's 'The Tyger', failed even to make the Top 10, while several votes were cast for poets that the organizers could not identify – perhaps attempts at poll rigging by the poets themselves, or their fans. A survey conducted by the BBC between 2 and 10 October 1996, which invited people to nominate only postwar poems, identified Jenny Joseph's 'Warning' as the nation's favourite.

DAILY NEWSPAPERS ON SALE
in the UK

	Newspaper	Average net circulation*
1	*The Sun*	3,060,447
2	*Daily Mail*	2,184,165
3	*Mirror*	1,289,067
4	*Daily Telegraph*	843,196
5	*Daily Express*	742,142
6	*Daily Star*	696,893
7	*The Times*	629,561
8	*Financial Times*	451,676
9	*Daily Record* (Scotland)	373,157
10	*The Guardian*	354,272

* 29 September–26 October 2008
Source: Audit Bureau of Circulations Ltd

LONGEST-RUNNING COMIC STRIPS
in British newspapers

	Strip	Newspaper	First appearance
1	Rupert Bear	*Daily Express*	8 Nov 1920
2=	The Broons	*Sunday Post* (Scotland)	8 Mar 1936
=	Oor Wullie	*Sunday Post* (Scotland)	8 Mar 1936
4	The Gambols	*Daily Express/Mail on Sunday*	16 Mar 1950
5	Andy Capp	*Daily/Sunday Mirror*	5 Aug 1957
6	Fred Bassett	*Daily Mail*	8 Jul 1963
7	George & Lynne	*The Sun*	Jul 1976
8	Beau Peep	*Daily Star*	2 Nov 1978
9	If...	*The Guardian*	2 Nov 1981
10	Striker	*The Sun*	11 Nov 1985

OLDEST PROVINCIAL NEWSPAPERS in the UK

Newspaper	First published
1 Berrow's Worcester Journal	c.1709
2 Lincoln, Rutland and Stamford Mercury	c.1710
3 Northampton Mercury and Herald	1720
4 Norwich Mercury	1726
5 Salisbury Journal	1729
6 Western Gazette (Yeovil, Somerset)	1737
7 News Letter (Belfast)	1738
8 Yorkshire Post (originally Leedes Intelligencer)	1754
9 Essex Chronicle	1764
10 Kentish Gazette	1768

Berrow's Worcester Journal, Britain's oldest surviving provincial newspaper, first appeared in 1690 as the Worcester Post-Man and later changed its name to Berrow's Worcester Journal. The Lincoln, Rutland and Stamford Mercury was originally published as the Stamford Mercury. The Kentish Gazette was originally called the Kentish Post or Canterbury News-Letter, 1717). Excluded here, the Press and Journal (Aberdeen), founded in 1922, incorporates two journals with earlier founding dates, the Aberdeen Daily Journal (1748), and the Aberdeen Free Press (1806).

GREAT
BRITISH
FARE

UNUSUAL BRITISH APPETITES

1   **George IV**
On 10 April 1830 the Duke of Wellington described a typical breakfast eaten by the grossly overweight king as consisting of a pie containing two pigeons and three steaks washed down with wine, Champagne, port and brandy. Two months later, he was dead.

2   **William Buckland**
Buckland (1784–1856), the eccentric Dean of Westminster, often served tortoise, rat and mouse on toast to his guests. He also devoured the mummified heart of Louis XIV.

3   **Frank Buckland**
Francis Trevelyan Buckland (1826–80), the son of William, ate monkey, zebra, crocodile, bear, grasshopper, giraffe, snake and elephant.

4   **Charles Darwin**
Darwin (1809-82) experimented with eating owl, armadillo and other rare creatures.

5   **William Forsyth**
Forsyth's Society for the Propagation of Horse Flesh as an Article of Food held a banquet in 1868 at which 160 guests ate a 10-course meal entirely derived from three horses.

6   **Vincent M. Holt**
Holt's book *Why Not Eat Insects?* (1885) contained such menus as Snail Soup, Fried Soles with Woodlouse Sauce, Curried Cockchafers, Fricassee of Chicken with Chrysalids, Cauliflowers garnished with Caterpillars and Moths on Toast.

7   **Edward VII**
Edward VII (1841–1910) customarily ate 14 courses for lunch *and* dinner, while the whole chicken placed beside his bed was invariably eaten down to its bones by the morning.

8   **Arthur Boyt**
Boyt (b. 1940), a retired entomologist of Davidstow, Cornwall, is a noted exponent of roadkill recipes, with ingredients that include bat, fox, owl, otter and badger.

9   **Peter Dowdeswell**
Dowdeswell (b. 1940) is considered the world's foremost speed eater and drinker, the holder of over 300 records, including 14 hard-boiled eggs in 14.42 seconds.

10   **Hugh Fearnley-Whittingstall**
The old-Etonian TV chef (b. 1965) is famous for consuming roadkill, human baby placenta and other unconventional ingredients.

PROTECTED GEOGRAPHICAL INDICATION British foods

1   Arbroath Smokies

2   Dorset Blue cheese

3   Herefordshire cider

4   Kentish ale

5   Rutland Bitter

6   Scotch beef

7   Scottish farmed salmon

8   Teviotdale cheese

9   Welsh lamb

10 Whitstable oysters

According to European Union regulations that came into force in 1993, Protected Geographical Indication (PGI) status is 'open to products which must be produced or processed or prepared within the geographical area and have a reputation, features or certain qualities attributable to that area'. Newcastle Brown Ale lost its PGI designation in 2007 when the brewery was relocated outside Newcastle. After 1 May 2009, all such products must display the PGI logo on their labels.

10

TRADITIONAL BRITISH DISHES

1   Beef Wellington
    The Duke of Wellington's connection with the beef Wellington – beef coated with paté and
    duxelles, wrapped in puff pastry and baked – is uncertain.

2   Christmas pudding
    The steamed fruit pudding originated in the medieval period, but was popularized in the
    Victorian era, especially through Dickens's description of it in *A Christmas Carol* (1843).

3   Haggis
    Although now associated with Scotland, haggis may have originated as early as the Roman
    period. It is an important feature of the Burns Supper, celebrated on 25 January.

4   Jellied eels
    Served with pie and mash, jellied eels are traditionally an East End of London dish, the
    earliest known eel and pie shop there dating from about 1850.

5   Lardy cake
    A kind of rich bread containing lard and dried fruit, it is thought to have originated in
    Wiltshire, but is also found in Sussex, Oxfordshire and Cambridgeshire.

6   Laver bread
    A Welsh bread made from seaweed, or laver, traditionally a breakfast dish eaten with bacon
    and cockles.

7   Pease pudding
    Familiar from the nursery rhyme *Pease Pudding (or Porridge) Hot*, it is composed of split
    peas made into a porridge.

8   Simnel cake
    Marzipan-covered fruit cake originally served on Mothering Sunday (the fourth Sunday in
    Lent), but now associated with Easter, its name comes from *simila*, the Latin for a fine flour.

9   Singing hinnies
    A Northumbrian griddle cake, so-called from the hissing sound made by the dough as it is
    dropped onto a hot griddle.

10 Stargazy pie
    A Cornish dish, said to originate in Mousehole where it is eaten on Tom Bawcock's Eve (23
    December), containing various fish including pilchards with their heads gazing starwards
    from the pastry crust. It was first described in 1847.

LOCALLY NAMED BRITISH DISHES

1   Banbury cakes
Resembling an oval Eccles cake (itself named after Eccles, Lancashire), they are claimed to have been made in Banbury, Oxfordshire, since 1586.

2   Bath chaps
One of several dishes associated with Bath, including Bath buns, Bath chine, Bath polony and Bath tripe. Bath chaps are the lower part of a pig's head, soaked in brine, simmered and rolled in breadcrumbs.

3   Bedfordshire clanger
Once eaten by agricultural labourers of the county, these comprise a suet pastry dish with meat filling at one end and jam in the other.

4   Brown Windsor soup
Despite its supposedly royal name and popularity in the Victorian and Edwardian period, this thick soup fell out of favour as a typical hotel and boarding-house course.

5   Cumberland pie
A dish resembling a shepherd's pie; the county also gave its name to Cumberland sausages and Cumberland sauce.

6   Dorset dumplings
Along with Dorset knobs, a biscuit, the county gave us this dish composed of apples served with suet.

7   Kendal mint cakes
The accidental invention in 1869 of Joseph Wiper, a Kendal confectioner, varieties of the mint cake are popular among climbers as a compact source of energy.

8   Malvern pudding
Deriving its name from Malvern, Worcestershire, it is a baked dish made from puréed apples and sugar, flavoured with lemon peel and cinnamon or nutmeg.

9   Melton Mowbray pork pie
First sold in 1831 by Edward Adcock, the pie was granted protected status in 2008, so that, under EU law, it may be made only in Melton Mowbray, Leicestershire.

10   Worcestershire sauce
Chemists John Wheeley Lea (1791–1874) and William Henry Perrins (1793–1867) are said to have first made the sauce in 1837, 'from a recipe of a nobleman in the county'.

TOP 10
TYPES OF CHEESE
in the UK

1   Cheddar

2   Blue cheese, including Stilton

3   Cheshire

4   Wensleydale

5   Red Leicester

6   Lancashire

7   Brie

8   Double Gloucester

9   Cornish Yarg

10   Goats' cheese

Source: British Cheese Board
Over 700 named cheeses are made in the UK, of which these were voted the nation's favourites in a 2008 poll conducted by the British Cheese Board. Some 540,000 tonnes of cheese are consumed annually in the UK, equivalent to 10.7 kg (23.6 lb) per person. Cheddar accounts for about 55 per cent (300,000 tonnes).

TOP 10

TYPES OF FISH EATEN
in the UK

	Fish	Tonnes*	Value
1	Nephrops (langoustine/scampi)	33,800,000	£84,000,000
2	Mackerel	120,600,000	£78,300,000
3	Haddock	47,600,000	£38,700,000
4	Scallops	20,700,000	£32,700,000
5	Monkfish	12,600,000	£30,600,000
6	Crabs	20,000,000	£23,700,000
7	Cod	13,800,000	£21,800,000
8	Herring	76,400,000	£15,900,000
9	Sole	1,800,000	£12,500,000
10	Whiting	8,900,000	£5,700,000
	Total (all species)	*458,300,000*	*£423,700,000*

* Landed by UK vessels, 2005
Source: Defra, *UK Sea Fisheries Statistics 2005*

10
BRITISH APPLE VARIETIES

	Apple	Cultivated by	Introduced
1	Ribston Pippin Hall,	Sir Henry Goodricke, Ribston Knaresborough, Yorkshire	1708
2	Blenheim Orange	George Kempster, Woodstock, Oxfordshire	*c.*1740
3	Bramley	Mary Ann Brailsford, Southwell, Nottinghamshire	*c.*1809
4	Cox's Orange Pippin	Richard Cox, Colnbrook, Berkshire	*c.*1830
5	Annie Elizabeth	Samuel Greatorex, Knighton, Leicestershire	1857
6	Egremont Russet	Lord Egremont, Petworth, Sussex	1872
7	Charles Ross	Welford Park, Newbury, Berkshire	1890
8	James Grieve	James Grieve, Edinburgh	1893
9	Laxton's Superb	Laxton Bros., Bedford	1897
10	George Cave	George Cave, Dovercourt, Essex	1923

SANDWICHES in the UK

Filling	Percentage of market
1 Chicken	30
2 Cheese, including ploughman's	14
3 Ham	9
4= Egg	8
= Tuna	8
6 Prawn	6
7 Bacon	5
8 Breakfast	4
9= Salmon	3
= Other meat	3

Source: British Sandwich Association
Some 2 billion sandwiches worth approximately £3.5 billion are purchased every year in the UK, while £3.86 billion are spent on lunchboxes containing a further 2.67 billion sandwiches. Among individual sandwich fillings, chicken salad accounts for 6.47 per cent of all sandwiches sold and chicken with bacon 5.97 per cent. Among more exotic fillings, hoisin duck has recently entered the Top 20. Outside the Top 10, beef and salad/vegetable each account for 2 per cent of the market and other fish/seafood 1 per cent. These use an estimated 24,924 tonnes of chicken, 10,576 tonnes of fish (3,505 of prawns, 4,735 of tuna and 1,783 of salmon), 6,816 tonnes of cheese, 7,790 tonnes of ham, 4,328 tonnes of bacon and 6,924 tonnes of eggs, accompanied by 135,300 tonnes of bread – about 98 million loaves. An additional estimated 6.24 billion sandwiches are made for consumption in British homes.

CRISP AND SNACK BRANDS
in the UK

1 Walkers original

2 McCoys

3 Pringles

4 Doritos

5 Hula Hoops

6 Quavers

7 Sensations

8 Kettle Chips

9 Mini Cheddars

10 Monster Munch

Source: ACNielsen
This list ranks 'impulse' purchases of Britain's most popular crisp and snack brands in convenience stores. Overall total retail sales figures for some British brands are a closely-guarded secret, but it is believed that Walkers crisps are worth £425 million a year, or £6.97 for every person in the country.

BESTSELLING BREAKFAST CEREALS in the UK

	Cereal*	Manufacturer	Percentage of retail market by value (2006)
1	Weetabix	Weetabix	7.71
2	Kellogg's Special K	Kellogg	6.13
3	Kellogg's Crunchy Nut	Kellogg	5.06
4	Kellogg's Corn Flakes	Kellogg	4.80
5	Shreddies	Cereal Partners	3.88
6	Kellogg's All Bran	Kellogg	3.53
7	Kellogg's Coco Pops	Kellogg	3.02
8	Cheerios	Cereal Partners	3.00
9	Kellogg's Rice Krispies	Kellogg	2.66
10	Kellogg's Frosties	Kellogg	2.58

* Named brands, excluding generic and supermarket own-brand products
Source: Euromonitor International, Global Market Information Database
Total breakfast cereal sales in the UK amount to over 1.3 million tonnes, with a retail value of £4.2 billion. Overall, Kellogg has a dominant 31.64 per cent of the market.

BESTSELLING BISCUITS
in the UK

	Biscuit*	Manufacturer	Percentage of retail market by value (2005)
1	McVitie's Digestive	United Biscuits	6.44
2	KitKat	Nestlé	5.26
3	Mini Cheddars	United Biscuits	4.57
4	Twix	Masterfoods	2.2
5	Penguin	United Biscuits	2.07
6	Cadbury Fingers	Burton's Foods	2.04
7	Maryland Cookies	Burton's Foods	1.68
8	Jammie Dodgers	Burton's Foods	1.53
9	McVitie's Hob-Nobs	United Biscuits	1.47
10	Blue Riband	Nestlé UK	1.41

* Named brands, excluding generic and supermarket own-brand products
Source: Euromonitor International, Global Market Information Database
Annual biscuit sales in the UK amount to almost 1.5 million tonnes, with a retail value of more than £4.4 billion. Purists will note the exclusion of Jaffa Cakes (a product of United Biscuits) from the Top 10. This follows a legal ruling that they are cakes and not biscuits – as a result of which, unlike chocolate-covered biscuits, VAT is not charged on them. The list here diverges somewhat from a recent OnePoll survey of favourites by type, which ranked Britain's favourite biscuits as: 1 Chocolate digestive; 2 Chocolate Hob-Nob; 3 Shortbread; 4 Chocolate chip cookie; 5 Custard cream; 6 Bourbon cream; 7 Hob-Nob; 8 Jammie Dodger; 9 Plain digestive; 10 Chocolate finger.

BESTSELLING BRANDS OF TEA
in the UK

	Tea*	Manufacturer	Percentage of retail market by value (2004)
1	PG Tips	Unilever Bestfoods	23.7
2	Tetley	The Tetley Group	22.1
3	Twinings	R. Twining	8.9
4	Typhoo	Premier Foods	5.2
5	Yorkshire	Betty & Taylors of Harrogate	4
6	Lyons	The Tetley Group	1.3
7	London Fruit & Herb	Premier Food Holdings	1
8	Teadirect	Cafédirect	0.8
9	Brooke Bond D	Unilever Bestfoods	0.7
10	Lift	Premier Foods	0.6

* Named brands, excluding generic and supermarket own-brand products
Source: Euromonitor International, Global Market Information Database
Tea sales in the UK amount to nearly 120,000 tonnes a year, of which 108,000 tonnes are black standard tea. The total value of all types of tea amounts to £1.57 billion per annum.

TOP 10

BESTSELLING FORTNUM & MASON LINES

1 Hampers

2 Royal Blend tea

3 Champagne truffles

4 Christmas puddings

5 Fortnum & Mason Blancs de Blancs Champagne

6 Royal Christmas cracker

7 Debrett's Correct Form (etiquette book)

8 Fortnum's Pickle

9 Piccadilly honey

10 Fortnum's Apron & Chef's Hat

Fortnum & Mason Ltd of Piccadilly dates from the early 18th century, when William Fortnum, a former footman in Queen Anne's household, joined forces with Hugh Mason to form a grocery store that soon became one of the most famous in the world. It was the first to stock the products of H. J. Heinz and has a long-standing reputation for producing food hampers, including, in 1985, the world's largest – a 2.7-cu.-m (96-cu.-ft) wicker basket of food and drink costing £20,000, which came complete with the services of a butler for one day!

FOOD AND DRINK BRANDS
in the UK

	Brand	Sales (2007)
1	Coca-Cola	£959,900,000
2	Warburtons bakery	£609,500,000
3	Walkers crisps	£424,500,000
4	Hovis bakery	£386,600,000
5	Cadbury Dairy Milk	£371,800,000
6	Nescafé instant coffee	£346,900,000
7	Lucozade	£337,700,000
8	Kingsmill bakery	£302,100,000
9	Robinsons soft drinks	£283,800,000
10	Tropicana	£245,900,000

Source: ACNielsen/*Checkout, Top 100 Grocery Brands 2007*

RESTAURANT TYPES
in the UK

	Type	Outlets	Annual sales
1	Various	16,222	£2,769,100,000
2	Indian	6,646	£1,886,600,000
3	Pizza	4,550	£946,700,000
4	Chinese	3,284	£707,900,000
5	Japanese	246	£66,600,000
6	Thai	695	£66,200,000
7	Mexican	190	£33,700,000
8	Indonesian/Malaysian/Singaporean	145	£16,400,000
9	Korean	54	£8,400,000
10	Vietnamese	60	£7,800,000

Source: Euromonitor, *Consumer Foodservice in the UK, 2005*

BRITISH RESTAURANTS
with two or more Michelin stars

Restaurant/location	Stars (2008)
1= The Fat Duck, Bray, Berkshire	***
= Restaurant Gordon Ramsay, London	***
= The Waterside Inn, Bray, Berkshire	***
4= The Capital Hotel, Knightsbridge, London	**
= Le Champignon Sauvage, Cheltenham, Gloucestershire	**
= Andrew Fairlie at Gleneagles, Auchterarder, Perthshire	**
= Le Gavroche, Mayfair, London	**
= Gidleigh Park, Chagford, Devon	**
= Le Manoir aux Quat'Saisons, Great Milton, Oxfordshire	**
= Midsummer House, Cambridge	**
= Pétrus, Berkeley Hotel, Knightsbridge, London	**
= Pied à Terre, Bloomsbury, London	**
= The Square, Mayfair, London	**
= The Vineyard at Stockcross, Newbury, Berkshire	**

The Michelin Guide to the British Isles was launched in 1911. The star rating, based on visits by a team of inspectors, was introduced in 1974, when 25 British restaurants received a single star. In 1977 four (Connaught, Le Gavroche, Waterside Inn and Box Tree) received two stars and in 1982 Le Gavroche became the first to be awarded three stars. This ultimate accolade signifies exceptional cuisine that is worth a special journey, two stars denote excellent cooking that is worth a detour and one star a very good restaurant.

TOP 10

MOST COMMON PUB NAMES
in the UK

	Pub name	Number
1	**Crown** Used for over 600 years, this symbol of royalty lost favour during Cromwell's period of power, but became popular again after the Restoration of the monarchy in 1660.	704
2	**Red Lion** Its earliest use represented the coat of arms of John of Gaunt, Duke of Lancaster (1340–99), the son of Edward III and the most powerful man in England for much of the 14th century. It is also a heraldic reference to Scotland.	668
3	**Royal Oak** Named after Charles II's attempts to escape the Roundheads by hiding in an oak tree.	541
4	**Swan** In use since the 1300s, it refers either to the bird or to a coat of arms.	451
5	**White Hart** King Richard II's heraldic symbol.	431
6	**Railway** Very popular since the railway-building boom of the 19th century.	420
7	**Plough** As well as the obvious farming reference, pub signs often depict the group of seven stars known as the Plough.	413
8	**White Horse** A widespread heraldic image.	379
9	**Bell** Church and hand bells have long been popular symbols.	378
10	**New Inn** This name was often given to a new pub that replaced an earlier one on the same spot.	372

Source: CAMRA (Campaign for Real Ale) survey, 2007

BRITISH PUB RECORD-HOLDERS

10

1 Oldest pub in Britain
Several pubs claim the title as Britain's oldest, among them Ye Olde Fighting Cocks, St Albans, Ye Olde Trip to Jerusalem, Nottingham, The Man and Scythe, Bolton, and The Bingley Arms, Bardsey.

2 Oldest pub in Wales
The Skirrid, Llanvihangel Crucorney, Abergavenny, is reputed to date from 1110, while, based on a reference in the writings of monk Giraldus Cambrensis, the Red Lion Inn, Llanfan Fawr, may have existed in 1188 or earlier.

3 Oldest pub in Scotland
Dating from 1734, the Clachan Inn on the Square, Drymen, claims to be the oldest pub in Scotland.

4 Oldest pub in London
The White Hart, Drury Lane, is said to have been first licensed as a public house in 1216.

5 Highest pub in Britain
The Tan Hill Inn, Arkengarthdale, Reeth, North Yorkshire, is situated at 528 m (1,732 ft).

6 Smallest pub in Britain
The Nutshell, Bury St Edmunds, Suffolk, occupies an area of 5 x 2m (16.5 x 6.5 ft).

7 Smallest pub in London
The Feathers, Linhope Street, Marylebone, lays claim to be the smallest pub in London.

8 Longest bar in Britain
The bar of the Horse Shoe, Drury Street, Glasgow, measures 32 m (104 ft).

9 Smallest bar in Britain
The Dove, Hammersmith, claims to have Britain's, if not the world's, smallest bar.

10 Most remote pub in Britain
The Old Forge, Knoydart by Mallaig, can be reached only by an 11-km (7-mile) ferry crossing or a 30-km (18-mile) mountain walk.

TOP 10
BRITISH PUBS
with the longest names

	Pub	Letters
1	Bertie Belcher's Brighton Brewery Company at the Hedgehog and Hogshead – It's Really in Hove, Actually* (Hove, East Sussex)	84
2	Henry J. Bean's but His Friends, Some of Whom Live Down his Way, All Call Him Hank Bar and Grill* (Fulham Road, London SW6)	74
3	The Royal Green Man and Blackamoor's Head Commercial and Family Hotel† (St John Street, Ashbourne, Derbyshire)	58
4	The Old Thirteenth Cheshire Astley Volunteer Rifleman Corps Inn (Astley Street, Stalybridge, Manchester)	55
5	The Fellows, Moreton and Clayton Brewhouse Company (Canal Street, Nottingham)	43
6	The Ferret and Firkin in the Balloon up the Creek* (Lots Road, London SW10)	40
7=	The London Chatham and Dover Railway Tavern (Cabul Road, London SW11)	37
=	The Footballers and Cricketers Public Arms (Linlithgow, Lothian)	37
9	The Argyll and Sutherland Highlander Inn (Eastham, Cheshire)	35
10	The Shoulder of Mutton and Cucumbers Inn‡ (Yapton, West Sussex)	34

* Defunct – other extant
† Full name; inn sign reads 'The Green Man and Black's Head'
‡ 'Inn' has recently been dropped from the name

No longer in use, the longest name here is one of the most recent of many – some more absurd than others – deliberately contrived to appear at the top of lists such as this ('Hove, actually . . .' is a phrase used by residents who object to being regarded as inhabitants of adjacent Brighton). There are a number of runners-up coincidentally containing 32 letters, including The Nightingale Theatre Public House, Brighton, East Sussex; The Queen Victoria and Railway Tavern, Paddington, London; The Worcestershire Brine Baths Hotel, Droitwich, Worcestershire; The Royal Gloucestershire Hussar Inn, Frocester, Gloucestershire and The Sir Gawain and the Green Knight Inn, Connah's Quay, Clwyd. The 24-letter I am the Only Running Footman, Charles Street, London W1, was for many years London's longest-named pub – running footmen were servants who ran alongside their employer's coach to clear the way and pay tolls; the last known exponent of this physically demanding profession worked for 'Old Q', the 4th Duke of Queensberry (1725–1810). The shortest-named pub in Britain was the now defunct X at Westcott, near Cullompton, Devon, but there have also been several with two letters, including the GI, Hastings, East Sussex, the XL Bar, Edinburgh, and the CB Hotel, Arkengarthdale, North Yorkshire.

TOP 10

OLDEST DISTILLERIES
in the UK

	Distillery	Founded/licensed
1	Bushmills, Antrim, Northern Ireland	1608
2	Bowmore, Isle of Islay	1779
3	Strathisla, Speyside	1786
4	Balblair, Edderton, Ross-shire	1790
5	Oban, Oban, Argyll	1794
6	Glen Garioch, Inverurie, Aberdeenshire	1797
7=	Ardbeg, Isle of Islay	1815
=	Laphroaig, Isle of Islay	1815
9	Lagavulin, Isle of Islay	1816
10	Bladnoch, Bladnoch, Dumfries and Galloway	1817

INDUSTRIOUS
BRITAIN

LOST BRITISH PROFESSIONS

1   Ale conner
The person who once tested ale or beer for quality and checked that the measures and prices at which it was sold were correct.

2   Climbing boy
Small children were once employed by chimney sweeps to climb inside flues. The dreadful life of one, Tom, is vividly described in Charles Kingsley's *The Water Babies* (1863) – even though the trade had been banned in 1840.

3   Crossing-sweeper
When horses were common on muddy city streets, crossing-sweepers received small payments for clearing a path to protect pedestrians' shoes and clothes. Jo in Dickens's *Bleak House* is a crossing-sweeper.

4   Gong farmer
Before modern plumbing, gong farmers or gong scourers emptied cesspits, ashpits and outside privies.

5   Knocker-up
In the days before alarm clocks were widely used, the knocker-up woke people on early shifts in factories – some by firing peas from peashooters at bedroom windows.

6   Postilion
The rider on a horse pulling a carriage – hence the (apocryphal) phrase attributed to a early foreign phrase book, 'My postilion has been struck by lightning'.

7   Pure collector
Collectors of dog droppings used in the leather tanning industry. Those employed in the trade were usually young girls or old women.

8   Ratcatcher
Ratcatchers generally used ferrets to drive them out of their holes and terriers to kill them.

9   Saggar-maker's bottom-knocker
Saggars are housings that protect pottery during firing in kilns, and their maker's assistant, who tested the bases by knocking them, was so-called. One such baffled the panellists on the TV quiz *What's My Line?*

10   Wang maker
A maker of small fastenings, such as buckles for shoes.

OLDEST-ESTABLISHED
BUSINESSES in the UK

	Business	Location	Founded
1	The Shore Porters Society of Aberdeen	Aberdeen	1498
2	Cambridge University Press (publishers)	Cambridge	1534
3	John Brooke and Sons (property management)	Huddersfield	1541
4	Whitechapel Bell Foundry	London	1570
5	Oxford University Press (publishers)	Oxford	1585
6	Richard Durtnell and Sons (builders)	Brasted, nr Westerham, Kent	1591
7	Tissimans & Sons Ltd (clothing)	Bishop's Stortford	1601
8	Hays at Guildford (office services)	Guildford (formerly London)	1651
9	*London Gazette* (journal)	London	1665
10=	Robert Noble (weavers)	Peebles, Scotland	1666
=	Spink (numismatists)	London	1666

The companies listed, and certain others, belong to an elite group of tercentenarians, firms that have been in business for 300 years or more. A few have even been under the control of the same family for their entire history. Although not a 'business', by some criteria the Royal Mint (founded in 886 in London, now relocated to Cardiff) may claim to predate all these enterprises.

BRITISH COMPANIES

	Company	Sector	Market value (2008)
1	Royal Dutch Shell	Oil and gas	£145,298,300,000
2	HSBC	Banking	£98,499,600,000
3	BP	Oil and gas	£96,525,100,000
4	Vodafone Group	Mobile telecommunications	£80,169,500,000
5	GlaxoSmithKline	Pharmaceuticals and biotechnology	£57,777,500,000
6	Rio Tinto	Mining	£52,215,100,000
7	Anglo American	Mining	£40,034,100,000
8	BG Group	Oil and gas	£39,024,900,000
9	British American Tobacco	Tobacco	£38,127,900,000
10	Xstrata	Mining	£34,482,300,000

Source: *Financial Times UK 500 2008*

BRITISH COMPANIES
with most employees

	Company	Employees (2008)
1	Compass Group	365,630
2	Tesco	345,754
3	HSBC Holdings	322,282
4	Royal Bank of Scotland	233,600
5	Royal Mail Holdings	198,704
6	Barclays	128,900
7	Anglo American	116,000
8	British Telecommunications	111,900
9	GlaxoSmithKline	103,483
10	J. Sainsbury	98,600

Source: *Fortune Global 500 2008*
This list includes only publicly quoted companies (companies whose shares are on the Stock Exchange). As well as these, the government and other organizations are major employers: the National Health Service, for example, employs about 1.3 million people, making it the largest employer in Europe and the 5th in the world (after the Chinese Army, Indian Railways, WalMart and the US Department of Defense).

LARGEST TRADE UNIONS
in the UK

	Union	Male	Membership* Female	Total
1	Unite	1,465,782	426,709	1,892,491
2	UNISON	403,200	940,800	1,344,000
3	GMB	325,981	264,088	590,069
4	Royal College of Nursing (RCN)	34,875	356,261	391,136
5	National Union of Teachers (NUT)	89,316	283,454	372,770
6	Union of Shop, Distributive and Allied Workers (USDAW)	150,374	205,672	356,046
7	Public and Commercial Services Union (PCS)	125,241	186,056	311,297
8	National Association of Schoolmasters Union of Women Teachers (NASUWT)	88,684	222,411	311,095
9	Communications Workers Union (CWU)	188,712	47,459	236,171
10	University and College Union (UCU)	61,635	55,276	116,911

* As at end of 2007, or latest year for which data available
Source: TUC
There are 193 trade unions in the UK with a total membership of 7,627,693. This contrasts with almost 500 unions and a membership of over 12 million 30 years ago, when there were still unions serving such bygone trades as glass bevelling and felt-hat making. The Card Setting Machine Tenters Society, with just 19 members, is Britain's smallest trade union.

BRITISH DUTY-FREE AND TRAVEL RETAIL SHOPS

	Location	World rank	2007 sales exceed
1	London Heathrow Airport	1	$1,000,000,000
2	London Gatwick Airport	10	$250,000,000
3	Manchester Airport	12	$250,000,000
4	P&O Ferries	20	$250,000,000
5	British Airways	33	$150,000,000
6	Stansted Airport	34	$150,000,000
7	Thomsonfly airline	68	$80,000,000
8	EasyJet airline	82	$60,000,000
9	Thomas Cook airlines	83	$60,000,000
10	Monarch Airlines	89	$50,000,000

Source: Generation Research

TOP 10

OLDEST-ESTABLISHED DEPARTMENT STORES in the UK

	Store/location*	Founded
1	Fortnum & Mason, London	1707
2	Boswells, Oxford	1738
3	Debenhams†, London	1778
4	Browns, Chester	1780
5	Joplings, Sunderland	1804
6	Heals, London	1810
7	Harvey Nichols, London	1813
8	Jarrolds, Norwich	1823
9	Austins, Derry, Northern Ireland	1830
10	Kendals, Manchester	1832

* Original store, excluding branches
† Founded as Flint & Clark, then Clark & Debenham, 1813, and Debenham & Freebody, 1851

LARGEST SHOPPING CENTRES
in the UK

	Shopping centre/location	Opened	Area
1	MetroCentre, Gateshead, Tyne and Wear	1986	165,000 sq m (1,776,000 sq ft)
2	Bluewater, Dartford, Kent	1999	155,700 sq m (1,675,940 sq ft)
3	Westfield London, Shepherd's Bush, London	2008	150,000 sq m (1,614,586 sq ft)
4	Westfield Merryhill, Dudley, West Midlands	1985	148,000 sq m (1,593,058 sq ft)
5	Trafford Centre, Trafford, Greater Manchester	1998	137,347 sq m (1,478,390 sq ft)
6	Meadowhall, Sheffield, South Yorkshire	1990	131,922 sq m (1,49,996 sq ft)
7	Lakeside, Thurrock, Essex	1990	130,300 sq m (1,402,537 sq ft)
8	Manchester Arndale, Manchester	1975	130,060 sq m (1,399,954 sq ft)
9	Liverpool 1, Liverpool, Merseyside	2008	130,050 sq m (1,399,846 sq ft)
10	St David's Centre, Cardiff, South Glamorgan, Wales	1982	129,561 sq m (1,394,852 sq ft)

10
ROYAL WARRANT HOLDERS*

	Company	Product
1	Cornelia James	Gloves
2	Flying Colours	Flags
3	W. Forbes	Taxidermy
4	Gibson Saddlers	Racing colours
5	Hunter Boot	Wellington boots
6	Kinloch Anderson	Kilts
7	Launer London	Handbags
8	Mars	Canned dog food
9	Marie O'Regan	Hats
10	James Purdey	Guns and cartridges

* **By Appointment to HM The Queen**
Royal Warrants are awarded to individuals and companies who have supplied goods or services for at least five years to The Queen (a total of 687), The Duke of Edinburgh (37) or The Prince of Wales (160). Warrant Holders are entitled to display the relevant Royal Arms and 'By Appointment' on their products, premises, stationery, vehicles and advertising.

BRITISH LOCAL INDUSTRIES

Town	Industry
1	Bridport, Dorset	Rope
2	Fletton, Cambridgeshire	Bricks
3	Hatton Garden, London	Jewellery
4	Loughborough, Leicestershire	Bells
5	Luton, Bedfordshire	Hats
6	Northampton, Northamptonshire	Shoes
7	St Helen's, Merseyside	Glass
8	Sheffield, Yorkshire	Cutlery
9	Stoke-on-Trent, Staffordshire	Pottery
10	Wilton, Wiltshire	Carpets

RICHEST BRITISH-BORN PEOPLE

	Name	Source of wealth	Net worth
1	The Duke of Westminster	Property	£7,000,000,000
2	Sir Philip and Lady Green	Retailing	£4,330,000,000
3	Sean Quinn	Property, etc.	£3,730,000,000
4	Earl Cadogan and family	Property	£2,930,000,000
5	Sir Richard Branson	Transport and mobile phones	£2,700,000,000
6	Joseph Lewis	Finance	£2,800,000,000
7	Bernie Ecclestone	Motor racing	£2,400,000,000
8	Jim Ratcliffe	Chemicals	£2,300,000,000
9	Alan Parker	Duty-free shopping	£2,086,000,000
10	Laurence Graff	Diamonds	£2,000,000,000

Source: *The Sunday Times Rich List 2008*

TOP 10

PORTS
in the UK

Port	Total traffic (2006)
1 Grimsby & Immingham	64,033,000 tonnes
2 Tees & Hartlepool	53,348,000 tonnes
3 London	51,911,000 tonnes
4 Southampton	40,556,000 tonnes
5 Milford Haven	34,306,000 tonnes
6 Liverpool	33,550,000 tonnes
7 Forth	31,556,000 tonnes
8 Felixstowe	24,370,000 tonnes
9 Dover	23,805,000 tonnes
10 Sullom Voe	19,447,000 tonnes
Top 10 total	*376,882,000 tonnes*
All UK ports	*583,739,000 tonnes*

Source: Department for Transport, *Transport Statistics Report, Maritime Statistics 2006*

FIRST BRITISH PATENTS

	Patentee	Patent	Date
1	Nicholas Hillyard	Engraving and printing the king's head on documents	5 May 1617
2	John Gason	Locks, mills and other river and canal improvements	1 Jul 1617
3	John Miller and John Jasper Wolfen	Oil for suits of armour	3 Nov 1617
4	Robert Crumpe	Tunnels and pumps	9 Jan 1618
5	Aaron Rathburne and Roger Burges	Making maps of English cities	11 Mar 1618
6	John Gilbert	River dredger	16 Jul 1618
7	Clement Dawbeney	Water-powered engine for making nails	11 Dec 1618
8	Thomas Murray	Sword blades	11 Jan 1619
9	Thomas Wildgoose and David Ramsey	Ploughs, pumps and ships' engines	17 Jan 1619
10	Abram Baker	Smalt (glass) manufacture	16 Feb 1619

The first patent in England dates from 1449, when John of Utynam was granted one by Henry VI for making glass for the windows of Eton College. Patents were occasionally granted during the 16th century, such as that issued in 1596 by Queen Elizabeth I to Sir John Harington for a water closet, but the system was not codified until 1617, and this list of the first 10 patents (in effect monopolies to exploit the devices) issued under the system gives some indication of the diverse range of inventions being developed even at this early date. It was not until 1852 that these patents were retrospectively numbered.

BIZARRE BRITISH PATENTS

BUSIEST RAILWAY STATIONS
in the UK

	Station/opened	Passengers entering or exiting*
1	London Waterloo (1848)	83,993,314
2	London Victoria (1862)	66,749,335
3	London Liverpool Street (1874)	55,265,748
4	London Bridge (1836)	47,576,684
5	London Charing Cross (1864)	34,779,287
6	London Paddington (1854)	27,258,741
7	London Euston (1837)	25,585,113
8	London King's Cross (1852)	22,503,777
9	London Cannon Street (1866)	21,106,127
10	Glasgow Central (1879)	21,002,296

* 2006–7
Source: Office of Rail Regulation
Although Clapham Junction, London, is often claimed to be Britain's busiest station, this is true only of the number of interchanges (12,898,160) made there; the actual number of passengers entering or leaving it was 18,868,026 in 2006–7.

MAKES OF CAR SOLD
in the UK

	Manufacturer	Sales (2007)
1	Ford	348,982
2	Vauxhall	331,321
3	Volkswagen	197,020
4	Peugeot	146,094
5	Renault	126,816
6	BMW	121,575
7	Toyota	118,493
8	Honda	106,018
9	Audi	100,864
10	Citroën	97,750
	Top 10 total	*1,694,933*
	Total cars sold	*2,404,007*

Source: Society of Motor Manufacturers and Traders Ltd

10 DEFUNCT BRITISH CAR MARQUES

1 Armstrong Siddeley
Siddeley Autocars, founded by John Davenport Siddeley in Coventry, merged with Armstrong Whitworth in 1919 and continued to make luxury cars until 1960.

2 Riley
Originally a Coventry bicycle manufacturer, the company was acquired in 1890 by William Riley. It made its first cars in 1905 and ceased production in 1969.

3 Humber
Humber was established in 1868 as a bicycle manufacturer by Thomas Humber, making its first car in 1898 and its last in 1975. French manufacturer Peugeot now owns the marque.

4 Wolseley
Herbert, later Lord Herbert Austin, made his first car in 1896. The Wolseley Motor Company dates from 1914, the marque continuing until 1975.

5 Hillman
The company was founded in 1907 by William Hillman. The last car bearing the Hillman badge was made in 1981. Peugeot now own the name.

6 Morris
William Morris, later Lord Nuffield, began making cars in 1910, merged his company with Austin in 1952 and ceased production in 1984.

7 Triumph
German-born Siegfried Bettmann and Moritz Schulte made their first cars in 1923, concluding with the Triumph Acclaim in 1984.

8 Talbot
The Talbot company dates from 1903 and merged with the Sunbeam marque in 1938. The marque was finally abandoned in 1986.

9 Austin
Herbert Austin set up his car company in Longbridge in 1905, introducing the mass-market Austin 7 in 1922 and the Mini in 1959. The Austin badge last appeared in 1987.

10 Reliant
Founded in Tamworth, Staffordshire in 1935, by former Raleigh Cycle Co. employee Tom Williams, the company made sports cars such as the Reliant Scimitar but was best known as the manufacturer of the three-wheeled Reliant Robin (1975–2002).

BRITISH BUSINESS AND INDUSTRY LASTS

1 Last of the Crystal Palace
Built in Hyde Park, London, in 1851 to house the Great Exhibition, the Crystal Palace was rebuilt at Sydenham. On 30 November 1936 it was totally destroyed by fire.

2 Last London tram
Originally horse-drawn (1860), then steam (1885), cable-drawn (1891) and finally electric (1901), London's last tram ran to the New Cross depot on 6 July 1952.

3 Last TV cigarette advertisement
A 60-second Rothmans International advert was the last to be screened in Britain on 31 July 1965, the day before a total ban came into force.

4 Last steam train
The last British Rail passenger steam train service in Britain, a return journey between Liverpool and Carlisle, shared between four locomotives, took place on 11 August 1968.

5 Last English pound note
First issued on 26 February 1797, the English pound note was replaced by the £1 coin and ceased to be legal tender on 12 March 1988. £1 notes continue in use in Scotland and the Channel Islands, and in 2008 the Lewes pound note was introduced in Lewes, East Sussex.

6 Last Durham coal mine
After over 800 years, Wearmouth Colliery, Sunderland, the last in the Durham coalfield, closed on 24 November 1993. The Stadium of Light football stadium was built on the site.

7 Last tin mine
Cornwall and Britain's last working tin mine, South Crofty, Camborne, in operation for over 400 years, closed on 6 March 1998.

8 Last Raleigh bicycle factory
Raleigh of Nottingham, once the world's largest bicycle manufacturer, was established in 1887. It closed its last factory on 28 November 2002.

9 Last British Airways Concorde flight
After being in service since 1975, the last scheduled transatlantic flight, from New York to London, took place on 24 October 2003.

10 Last building society
As a result of the economic turmoil of 2008, Bradford & Bingley, Britain's last independent building society, was part nationalized, with its savings arm being acquired by Abbey.

ACKNOWLEDGEMENTS

Paul Donnelley
Brian Durrans
Cornell Kimball
Ian Morrison
Tim O'Donovan
Dafydd Rees
Robert Senior

artnet
Association of Leading Visitor Attractions
Association of National Park Authorities
Audit Bureau of Circulations Ltd
BBC
The Bereavement Register
British Birds
British Cheese Board
British Library
British Sandwich Association
British Toy Retailers Association
British Video Association
British Waterways
CAMRA
Checkout
Department for Environment, Food and
  Rural Affairs
Department for Transport
Department of Health
Design Museum
The Economist
Emporis
Euromonitor International
Financial Times
Forestry Commission
Fortune
GB Non-native Species Secretariat
Generation Research
General Register Office for Scotland
*The Grim Reaper's Road Map: An Atlas of
  Mortality in Britain* (Mary Shaw, *et al*, 2008)
HBOS
Imperial War Museum
International Time Capsule Society
Internet Movie Database

www.karaokeinfo.co.uk
The Kennel Club
London Eye
The Man Booker Prize
The Met Office
Ministry of Justice
Movie Information Database
Music Information Database
National Amusement Park Historical
  Association
National Association for Areas of
  Outstanding Natural Beauty
National Federation of Women's Institutes
National Piers Society
National Statistics
National Trust
AC Nielsen
Northern Ireland Statistics and Research
  Agency
Office for Rail Regulation
Office of Health Economics
The Official UK Charts Company
www.Onepoll.com
Ordnance Survey
Oscar Pet Foods
Oxford English Dictionary
Performing Right Society
Pet Food Manufacturers' Association
Royal Opera House
Royal Society for the Prevention of Cruelty
  to Animals
Screen Digest
Shakespeare Centre
Society of Motor Manufacturers and
  Traders Ltd
Sunday Times
Trades Union Congress
HM Treasury
UK Intellectual Property Office
United Nations Educational, Scientific and
  Cultural Organization
Who Owns Britain (Kevin Cahill, 2001)
World Conker Championships